TRAINING GROUND

SHANNON HALTOM

Training Ground

Trilogy Christian Publishers
A Wholly Owned Subsidiary of Trinity Broadcasting Network
2442 Michelle Drive, Tustin, CA 92780

10 9 8 7 6 5 4 3 2 1
Library of Congress Cataloging-in-Publication Data is available.

ISBN: 979-8-89333-073-1
E-ISBN: 978-8-89333-074-8

DEDICATION

I dedicate this book to my children, Jacob and Gracen Haltom. May you run the race God has marked out for you with patient endurance. May you continue to hear from the living God yourself and know who He is. I pray you never lose your tenacious desire to press forward for the Kingdom of God.

> *Therefore, since we are surrounded by such a great cloud of witnesses, let us throw off everything that hinders and the sin that so easily entangles. And let us run with perseverance the race marked out for us, fixing our eyes on Jesus, the pioneer and perfecter of faith. For the joy set before him he endured the cross, scorning its shame, and sat down at the right hand of the throne of God.*
>
> —Hebrews 12:1–2 NIV

ACKNOWLEDGMENTS

Thank You to my Creator, Jesus Christ. He first and foremost gets the glory. Thank you to my husband, Bo, and my children, Gracen and Jacob, for supporting me in my desire to run both physically and for the Kingdom. It is because of your support that training is even possible. Thank you, Coach Jason Llanes, for developing the running plan, for your encouragement along the way, and for holding me accountable to my miles each day/week. Thank you, Pastors Paul and Becki Stieb, for your prayers and your spiritual accountability. Thank you for pouring into me and loving me for who I am, for being willing to put me in a position that would propel me toward my destiny.

Thank you to my parents, George and Stacey Silvas, for your continued belief and intercession for me—that is worth more than gold. Finally, thank you to Brenda George, my spiritual mother, the woman who pulled out the God in me, who has seen me at my best and loved me at my worst. Even in my raw state, you loved me with grace and humility. No words could ever express the amount of love I have for you. You are my Elijah.

CONTENTS

FOREWORD

There are several things I believe I'm right about when it comes to Shannon. One, she's not perfect, but she *does* know the Perfect One, Jesus. And two, deep down inside, she desires to live for Him. And whether she's always followed His plan for her life or not, she knows His plan is better than hers.

God has a plan for *every* person on the planet—a race for us to run. He created us with a purpose in mind—and not just any purpose, but an exciting, unique, God-given purpose. We are chock-full of potential—God potential. Hidden inside each of us is a destiny just waiting to meet with us.

It's the life everyone is searching for; they just don't know it. When you break it all down, we all want the same thing. We just want to be happy. In the Bible, *happy* is another word for *blessed*. And this is exactly how God intended for us to live.

Our Creator has already put the plan together and mapped out for us the path it's going to take to get there. Now it's up to us to take the steps.

If you've ever planned a surprise party for someone you really love, you know the excitement you feel, knowing what's in store for them. A few years ago, I had the pleasure of planning a surprise birthday party for my husband, Paul. Since we're pastors and his birthday fell on a Sunday, I thought it would be a great idea to celebrate his birthday at church. I can't begin to tell you how much joy it brought to me that day, and even now, two years later. Just thinking about it makes me happy all over again.

I have to say, it was one of my favorite Sunday services ever! He had no idea what was in store for him—but *I did*. I knew what I had planned for him, and I couldn't wait for him to experience it. The day finally arrived, and it was absolutely amazing. Watching him soak everything in with such awe as the day unfolded, with one surprise after another, was priceless. The party was for *him*, but I felt like, somehow, I got in *good* on his blessing. There's just something about seeing someone you love so happy.

I had planned this amazing party, and I had strategically put all of the pieces together and the people in place to help it come to pass. I was sitting on the edge of my seat the whole time, in anticipation of what was to come. It was quite something to see the plan unfold and to see Paul's life touched in a way he will never forget. That day left an indelible mark. It was so worth it. Even though he had no idea what was in store for him, *I knew*—and I couldn't wait for him to experience it… *all* of it!

I believe this must be how our heavenly Father feels about what is in store for us. He has put together, for each one of us, an amazing plan (Jeremiah 29:11). We have no idea what all He has in store for us (1 Corinthians 2:9), but *He does*. And I believe He sits on the edge of His seat, in anticipation of what's to come. He knows what He has planned for us, and He can't wait for us to experience it.

How it must bless Him to see us walking in all the things He's prepared for us. What joy it must bring Him to watch us soak in His goodness as we run the race He's marked out for us to run... a race all our own... a race that leads to blessings, not only for us, but for others.

The Father has strategically mapped out the path and put all the pieces together and the people in place to help it come to pass. It's like He's planned this amazing surprise party for us called Life, and He can't wait for us to experience it... *all* of it! The party's for us, but it brings God such joy to see us so blessed. There's just something about seeing someone He loves so happy.

In her book *Training Ground*, Shannon has taken the analogy of a natural race, with all the things needed to run it successfully, to illustrate the importance of those things when it comes to your spiritual race. These things include preparation, believing in yourself, trusting those who have successfully gone before you, and trusting and embracing the process along the way. Though many would love to bypass the process, it would be to their detriment. The process is what forges in us the very things we need to experience and sustain the blessings of God.

Shannon reminds us that everything in life doesn't come easy, that it takes work, tenacity, self-discipline, and character to keep moving forward in life. Most of all, she reminds us that we need Someone bigger than ourselves to be truly successful, and beyond that, to be significant. We need Jesus. Because, you see, this life is not about us; it's all about Him. And because of that, everything we do should revolve around *Him*. We are on this earth to love God and to love other people. And we need to know that every decision we make doesn't just affect us; it affects others. That's why every decision we make matters.

God has some amazing plans for your life. And He wants you to enjoy them not just for a moment, but rather, for a lifetime. But in order for that to happen, you're going to have to be willing to allow Him to build in you the character you will need to sustain those remarkable plans.

I encourage you to delve into the Scriptures Shannon has highlighted in this book and allow God to speak to you personally. Get to know who God is and who you are in Him. Train hard and keep training. Then focus on the prize and start running your God race. Start running and never stop. Run like your life depends on it—because it does. Keep training. Keep running. Do it for God. Do it for yourself. Do it for your children and your children's children. Do it for the world, which is in desperate need of a Savior.

The party has been planned, the invitation has been sent, and He awaits your RSVP.

Pastor Becki Stieb
Rescue Church

INTRODUCTION

THE WARMUP

Growing up, I hated running (I have a story for that later), but as I am becoming the woman God has called me to be, He has placed a passion in me for running. Today, I love to run. In the fall of 2020, I had a fresh desire to run a marathon (26.2 miles). I know it sounds crazy, right?

My love for physical fitness and endurance came about three years ago, when God placed a dream in my heart to climb mountains and travel the world for His purposes. I knew that to do what He was calling me to do and be effective, I had to do my part to get healthy and be in my best physical shape. I joined a CrossFit gym and made running a part of my routine. Little did I know that through my training, God would reveal to me how running physically is so closely related to running for Him spiritually in this race called life.

After sharing my passion and desire to run a full marathon with my coach, our plan was to start training—he wanted to take the training slow, but I wanted it "now." After suffering a knee injury due to my impatience, I had to postpone my training and even cease running for a season. My impatience cost me.

One year later, in August 2021, I decided to start training again. This time, I would do it differently. I waited for my coach to write out a plan that would help me reach my goal. As I reviewed the plan, I was overwhelmed and anxious about how I would fit in the running each day along with everything else! The one thing I had going for me was that I was in charge of my schedule, so that should certainly give me a leg up. However, I also was still extremely busy with being a wife, mom, entrepreneur, and volunteer. I recalled a Scripture that helped me refocus my priorities:

> *But seek ye first the kingdom of God, and his righteousness; and all these things shall be added unto you.*
>
> —Matthew 6:33 KJV

On day one of training, I woke up earlier than normal to spend time with the Lord. Now, quiet time for me, or spending time reading the Bible and listening for God to speak, is something I was doing quite regularly, but here in recent months, let's admit it: I had been slacking.

My life was in the middle of a transition with my career, entrepreneurship, and ministry. I had recently left my cushy corporate career to take a step of faith and start my own company. I had also said "yes" to taking on the youth ministry for an interim season at our church on top of other ministry duties for which I was responsible. Oh yes, and don't forget that small detail of being a wife and mom. My plate was full! I know, I know—before you judge me, let me just say I am not perfect, but I had put my time with the Lord on the back burner to whenever I could get to it.

This particular morning, I was not sure how I was going to get a short two-mile run in based on the busyness of my calendar. Nevertheless, I woke up and made the conscious decision to put my time with the Lord first. When the clock struck 4:45 a.m., I drove to CrossFit for training. The workout that morning was fairly quick, and I had time left to spare, just enough time to run two miles. Off I went. As I was out for this two-mile run, I heard the Holy Spirit whisper so gently, *Shannon, you see how you put Me first and sought to spend time with Me this morning? When you put Me first, I will make sure that everything else falls into place for you. I know that running is important to you. I know that training is important to you, and because it is important to you, it is important to Me. The training and the running is not just for you, but it is for the Kingdom. I have a purpose for it. If you continue to put Me first, I will make sure that everything else falls into place for you.*

Wow! God was speaking to me while I was running—and guess what? He was not done. The conversation didn't end there. He went on to tell me that there was a reason I hadn't trained the previous year—it wasn't the right time. He needed me to train now during this season because He was about to teach me that not only was I embarking on physical training for a natural race, but He was also placing me in spiritual training for a supernatural race. I just had to lean in and trust Him. Will you lean in and trust Him, too?

The apostle Paul tells us:

*Do you not know that in a race all the runners run
[their very best to win], but only one receives the
prize? Run [your race] in such a way that you may
seize the prize and make it yours! Now every athlete
who [goes into training and] competes in the games is
disciplined and exercises self-control in all things. They
do it to win a crown that withers, but we [do it to
receive] an imperishable [crown that cannot wither].
Therefore, I do not run without a definite goal; I do
not flail around like one beating the air [just shadow
boxing]. But [like a boxer] I strictly discipline my body
and make it my slave, so that, after I have preached
[the gospel] to others, I myself will not somehow be
disqualified [as unfit for service].*

—1 Corinthians 9:24–27 AMP

I had no idea what God was about to show me through this training, but I knew the vision was bigger than just training for a physical marathon. God has divinely ordered these chapters that He has denoted as "miles." For every mile I have trained, I have listened intently for the voice of my heavenly Father, earnestly leaning in for the lesson He wanted to teach me. I hope to impart the wisdom from the lessons I have learned throughout my training to you, so that you may run the race God has prepared for you. I pray you are not just motivated, but inspired to run your God-given race and fulfill your destiny. Whether you like to physically run or not doesn't matter—if you desire to reach your destiny and fulfill your calling, then this book is for you. Think of this *Training Ground* as a journey you are on in life; it is a marathon, not a sprint. What I have learned is that we are in constant training, and we will be until the Lord calls us home. How far we get in our training is up to us.

In this training ground of life, there are trials, there are highs and there are lows, there are losses and there are gains, but one thing I can promise is that there is victory. The training is the process you must go through to reach and fulfill the God-given purpose and destiny that He has for you. It is not easy, and it is not for the faint of heart, but it is worth it. Much like the physical process of running and training for an actual race, there is a spiritual process for which you must endure and train to reach your destiny. Can I encourage you? The process is worth it. Whether you find yourself just starting, restarting, on the mountaintop celebrating a win, or in the valley grieving a loss, our Creator wastes nothing. He uses every ounce of training to build you up into the unique individual you were designed to be. This training has a Kingdom purpose with a Kingdom agenda, and it is directly connected to our God-given races—both yours and mine. God has a plan for each of our lives—even for you.

> *"For I know the plans I have for you," declares the*
> Lord, *"plans for welfare and not for evil, to give you*
> *a future and a hope."*
>
> —Jeremiah 29:11

In today's culture and society, we are rushed. We are pressed for time. We are moving at a fast pace, and we want everything to be tangible at our fingertips with a touch of a button. Yet the one thing we cannot rush is the process. God has a race for you that only you can run, and it cannot be completed overnight. It cannot be "microwaved," and it will not happen any faster than it is supposed to. God's plan is a process and will not be rushed. My prayer for you is that by the end of this book, you will be inspired to embrace your training ground with tenacity and fervor, to run with endurance and fulfill the purpose God has for you. Run your race to be effective for the Kingdom of God and leave a legacy with a firm foundation for generations to come.

At the end of each "mile," you will find a few questions to help you make the most of your training ground. Feel free to write in the margins, dog-ear the pages, and take lots of notes. Also, in case you are interested, I have put my personal training plan for running a marathon at the end of the book.

Get ready. Get set. Let's run!

MILE 1
OBEDIENCE

What is your greatest obstacle? What keeps you from moving forward toward your destiny? In my experience of mentoring and speaking to many different individuals about their purpose, the biggest obstacle is always obedience to the process of preparation. Everyone wants the mountaintop experience, yet few are willing to go through the process of preparation to get to it. Process is where most find themselves stuck. Preparation is what most find difficult. Why? Because the process is painful, ugly, and just plain hard at times. Preparation takes work. Mile 1 is *obedience*. Let that word sink in. We are starting with obedience on the front end because obedience will be required of you to even start your training. This is *Training Ground*.

When you first hear the word *obedience*, the thought of draconian laws, rules, and regulations may come to mind. The word itself is strong. The thought of someone shaking a stick at you and laying down a bunch of "thou shalts" might be a bit of a turnoff. Obedience doesn't have to sound legalistic and controlling, though. While God sets the standard and provides us with guidelines that we should live within, like the Ten Commandments, they are not there to lock us in a box, nor to punish us. Quite the opposite, they are there to protect us, to free us, and to bless us. There is power in obedience. Think of it this way: If you have a small child at home and you are cooking in the kitchen with the stove on, you would tell the child not to touch the stove because it could burn them. You know what could happen if the child chose not to obey your command and touch the stove. You didn't give the command to punish them; you gave it to protect them. Like this, God gives us boundaries to protect us. Obedience is what brings your blessing into reality. Obedience to what? you might ask. Obedience to the call. Obedience to the last directive. Obedience to the direction. Obedience to the instruction. Obedience to the command. Obedience to the Word of God. Obedience precedes the blessing. Oftentimes, we think we are waiting on God to move, when all actuality, He is waiting on us to do what He has already asked us to do.

There are many examples in the Bible that prove obedience must come first. For example, David was a man after God's own heart; he was obedient to both the Word of God and the call. Daniel was obedient to fasting and praying before he was rescued from the mouths of the lions. Shadrach, Meshach, and Abednego were obedient to worship God alone, and for that, they were rescued from the fire. The apostle Paul was obedient to the call, pressing forward under pressure to run his race and went on to write over half of the New Testament. There is power in obedience. Obedience is what causes God to move on your behalf. He is faithful. Does that mean you won't experience challenges when you are obedient? No—instead, you are more likely to experience them. There is a story tucked away in

Mark 4:35–41, where we find Jesus and His disciples in a boat going across the sea to the other side, when out of nowhere arose a great storm. The disciples were in the will of God. Jesus gave the instruction, "Let us go to the other side," and the disciples obeyed by getting into the boat and journeying to the other side. On the way, a storm arose. When you are in the boat of obedience (the Father's will), there will be challenges, pressures in life, and trials, but that is what we call process. The process of walking out your obedience brings pressure and process itself, which God uses to strengthen your resolve and faith in Him. Trust Him *through* the process.

When you think about spiritual giants (great men and women of faith), whether in the Bible or here physically, they didn't get there without obedience and process. As we endure the process of preparation, there are a few key pieces to which I want to draw your attention in which God requires obedience so we can experience Him.

SEPARATION

Before God takes us to the next level, He will often call us to a season of separation. If we aren't careful, we won't recognize what it is, and we will miss out on the opportunity to maximize the season. As I write this book to you, I find myself in the process of separation. I didn't realize it until now, but God has been trying to separate me for a different reason: to draw me closer to Him.

Let me explain. After nearly fifteen years of working in health care, I transitioned to entrepreneurship. For the last several months, I have also been enveloped with shifting my focus to spending more time at home being a wife and mother. What I know now is that God called me to a season of separation: Separation from what I used to associate myself with. Separation from a title and position. Separation to allow space for Him to sustain me, exceed my expectations, and reveal Himself to me in new ways. This season of separation looks a lot different than what I expected, but it is honestly my best season yet.

Separation can bring about many different emotions. For instance, it can cause you to feel isolated and alone. You may experience a sense of loss or an uncomfortable feeling of uncertainty. God separates you so you will spend more time with Him. He desires to get you away from distractions and the things on which you were once dependent and viewed as "normal" in your life. He knows that to take you to the next level in Him, you have to be willing to let go of some things to make room for the new. You need Him. He knows you need Him. He will pull you aside from what you're used to so you can experience Him, and then He will use you as His mouthpiece. God will separate you from different situations, people, and places so He can do the inner work in you that's needed to prepare you for the next season. It wasn't until I separated myself through obedience that I was able to dedicate time to train for a marathon. After taking this step of faith, I was able to dedicate time to writing this book you hold in your hands. In fact, this book wasn't even a thought in my mind until well after I made the transition. I believe God waits for us to take the first step of faith in obedience to Him before He reveals the next step in His plan. Too often, we want all the steps to be revealed in advance, but God doesn't work that way; He works in steps and stages. What step of obedience is God asking you to take?

There are many patriarchs in the Bible whom God called to be separated from the pack and go to a place of solitude so He could do an inner work to prepare them for the next season. For instance, Elijah was separated at Cherith to experience God as Provider before his famous Mount Carmel experience (1 Kings 17). David was anointed king as a boy, yet he was sent back to the field to oversee his father's sheep, separate from everyone else, before he could take his place as king. During that time in the field, David learned how to defend the sheep. He learned how to fight. He learned how to draw near and experience God for himself, long before his public defeat of Goliath (1 Samuel 16).

I am a firm believer that God does His best work in the dark. When we don't see it, He is working. I love that He works on us in obscurity and trains us when no one is watching. Training is the part no one sees. From what is God trying to get you to separate yourself? Hear me correctly: God wouldn't call you to separate yourself from something that contradicts His Word, like your spouse. He would separate you from a group of people who are a distraction for you, who keep you from following His Word. He would call you to separate yourself from anything that has gotten in the way of your relationship with Him. He may be calling you to separate yourself from a certain place. Whatever the season of transition is for you, I pray that

23

you seek wise counsel, pray earnestly, follow peace, and have faith to be obedient.

SACRIFICE

Preparation and obedience in the process will always require a sacrifice. Your anointing will cost you. Your destiny will cost you. There is a sacrifice required of you, your time, your talent, and your treasure.

TIME

This is the one currency of which we all have equal amounts, yet none of us has control over it. When I was in nursing school, our class was very small, so we all were relatively close-knit and developed study groups. We had a slogan we would share as we prepared for every test: "We Need More Time!" One of our classmates had T-shirts made with this slogan when we graduated. The truth is, no one gets more time. The only element we can control is how we invest the time we *are* given. During your training, you have to be willing to say "no" to good things, so you can "yes" to the God thing. When you say "yes" to the God thing, you can focus your energy in the right place. You may have to give up going to gatherings on the weekends so you can go on long runs or write that book that has been hidden in your heart for the last ten years. I spent seven months training for the marathon. Each week, I chose to put in hours of training every week. As race day approached, I had nearly fifteen to twenty hours a week invested in my training. I had to choose to invest time to train. You will prioritize your time based on what you value. How you steward your time matters.

TALENT

God placed talents and gifts on the inside of each of us. Now, when He put it there, it wasn't fully developed. He placed it there in seed form; it is up to us to water it (practice it), develop it, and use it for His glory. Talents and gifts are unique to all of us. I wouldn't say that running is my "talent." I am certainly not fast, but in this season of training, God pulled the writing gift out of me, the gift of communication. This book is my seed that hopefully will bring forth fruit in your life. God is so good that He didn't create us all the same. I am thankful for that. I am thankful that there are people who have talents in singing so they can lead us in worship. I am thankful that there are people with talents in finance and business skills on whom we can lean to help steward resources and investments well. I can't help but wonder how many people aren't using the talents they were given because they have forgone their development. When you sacrifice your time to use your talents for the Kingdom of God, the seed grows, develops, and matures, maximizing your potential. What talent do you have that you have not practiced and surrendered to the Lord for His glory?

TREASURE

Now, most people associate treasure with money, because that seems to be the world's focus, and let's face it, people get funny when you talk about money, especially in church. Now that's the truth! You can talk about money anywhere and at any place, but the second you talk about money in church, the church people act funny. Here's the truth, though: "Where your treasure is, there will your heart be also" (Luke 12:34). So, where is your heart? Is your heart seeking monetary gain or the Kingdom? What is your motive? Our motive for serving has to be right. You cannot outgive God. God doesn't need your money. If you seek the Kingdom, and follow God's principles on giving, the money will follow. That's the way God's economy works. For anything for which you want to train, prepare, or endure, it is going to cost you. It costs you something—and not just dollars. It costs you blood, sweat, and tears. God will prepare you to sacrifice your treasure, increase your giving, and test your generosity, and if you are willing to let it go for His sake, He will bring it back with interest.

SELF-DISCIPLINE

Self-discipline is a key ingredient for any training, especially your spiritual training. In fact, I believe it is so important that you will see this topic again layered throughout the book. You have to be willing to do the small, mundane things every day if you want to see the results and experience the growth for which you are looking. If you will be obedient in this season, you will have gained self-discipline, character, and the ability to endure what you will face in the next season. Each training season builds and prepares you for the next. You have to be willing to train in this season, even when you don't feel like it. One of the very first conversations my coach and I had prior to the start of the training was concerning self-discipline. He said it this way: "Shannon, you will have to make up your mind to decide that you will run, even when you do not feel like it. You will have to decide now to run regardless of the circumstances, whether it is hot or cold, whether it is raining or dry."

> But I discipline my body and keep it under control, lest after preaching to others I myself should be disqualified.
>
> —1 Corinthians 9:27

This is what the apostle Paul meant when he said he disciplined his body. Your body will want to quit. There will be days when your body does not want to run. There will be days when your body does not want to train, but you will have to have already prepared yourself—mentally and spiritually—in advance, with what you will tell your body when the time comes: *Body, you will submit to the training process.*

We recently celebrated my grandmother's birthday, and the dessert table was filled with red velvet cake with cream cheese icing and homemade powdered sugar cookies with pecans. I was doing my best to refrain from even taste-testing, yet in all the peer pressure to "just have one," I said, "That's my problem—I can't just have one. I already know that if I start, I will want more." Then I was reminded by my dad, "Don't you have self-control? You are supposed to tell your body, *Body, you are just having one.*" Well, that sounded good and authoritative, but after one turned into five… sometimes, the self-discipline is to just refrain altogether.

The self-discipline it takes to refrain from the cake and sugar cookies is the same self-discipline that it takes to get up and train, to push through the hard stuff, to forgive those who have betrayed you, and to love when you don't feel like it. In what is God asking you to be more disciplined?

There is power in obedience. Obedience to the separation, sacrifice, and self-discipline are required for your training ground. For you to go to the next season, you have to finish the assignment you were given in this season. With what instruction or directive are you struggling? What has God asked you to separate yourself from so you can experience Him? What has God spoken to you in a sweet whisper, what is His latest instruction to which you need to step forward in obedience? Remember, obedience precedes the blessing. God's love for us is unconditional. There is nothing you have to do to earn His love or His grace. It is freely given. However, God's promises are conditional. To experience the promise, it requires a step of obedience from you. If I were sitting next to you while you are reading these words, this is where I would lean in and say, "Your ticket to eternity has already been paid for, but if you want to experience heaven on earth, that requires obedience."

Maybe you are reading this, and you have never done this "Jesus Thing" before. Before we go any further, allow me to introduce Him to you.

For God so loved the world, that he gave his only Son,
that whoever believes in him should not perish but
have eternal life.

—John 3:16

The Son is Jesus Christ, who gave His life for you and me, who paid for all our sins—past, present, and future—so we could have eternal life. If we believe in our hearts and confess with our mouths, we will be saved (Romans 10:9). When you make the decision to believe in Jesus and make Him the Lord of your life, it is the single best decision you will ever make. It is that simple. Pray this prayer with me:

Dear Lord,
   Thank You for dying on the cross for me and
raising from the dead to give me eternal life. Forgive
me of my sins and make me new. From this day
forward, I choose to confess that You are the Lord of
my life.
   In Jesus' name, amen.

From here, I encourage you to find a Bible-based church you can attend and to start reading your Bible. Reading the Bible doesn't have to be complicated. Find a version that you can understand. There are even electronic and audio versions. Whatever works for you, just start.

TRAINING QUESTIONS

1. From what is God calling you to separate yourself so you can dive deeper into your relationship with Him?

2. What step of obedience are you being asked to take?

3. In which element are you currently making a sacrifice? Which is the hardest and why?

   a. Time

   b. Talent

   c. Treasure

4. In what area of life do you need to develop self-discipline? What is holding you back?

MILE 2

REFOCUS

I am so blessed to have amazing pastors who have poured into me, pulled gifts out of me, and positioned me to propel forward. I knew deep down in my heart that I was becoming lukewarm. I could tell in my words, in my attitude, and in the results I was delivering. Yet I didn't want to admit it. I wanted to still look like I had it all together.

During one of our ministry training sessions, my pastors loved me enough to tell me that the lukewarm temperature I was feeling was showing. Not in these exact words, but close enough: "Let's admit it, there's water on your fire."

Ouch! My flesh wanted to be offended, and I thought, *I am fine. No one has to tell me about my walk with Jesus. I've got it under control. I mean, do you know what all I am juggling? I think I am doing pretty darn good.* Let me be clear, I did not say that out loud, but I thought it—because our minds are quick to be defensive. Yet, rather than allow my flesh to get carried away, I immediately did a heart check. I knew where that wrong thinking was coming from. The enemy was planting seeds of pride and offense to create division—exactly what happens when you become lukewarm. The enemy would love for you to get offended, walk away, quit, and abort your destiny. I had become easy prey.

Our God is so sovereign, though, that even in that moment, it was a setup for me. What was most revelatory was that I also felt the sting of conviction from the Holy Spirit. My pastors were right. I could blame putting God on the back burner on any number of things, but all of it would be an excuse. I needed to take responsibility for my relationship with God and do my part. No one was in charge of my schedule but me. No one is in charge of my spiritual walk but me. I decide. So I made the decision to get my fire back. For those of you who are not in ministry and you are reading this, you are probably thinking, *How can someone who is in church and overseeing different ministries lose their fire or put God on the back burner?* It's simple: We are human just like you, and we are not immune from the attacks of the enemy. We have the same skin suit and the same life challenges you do. There is a difference between studying the Bible to prepare a message for people, compared to just sitting in worship, seeking to spend time with the Father for yourself. The latter is where I needed an adjustment. For those of you who *are* in ministry, you know exactly what I am talking about, and my prayer for you is that you seek your First Love and finish strong. I am praying for you. I pray that you surround yourself with people who will love you enough to be honest and confront you in hard areas, so that you can grow and stretch in those difficult places—because, like me, you, too, have to decide. You either want to grow or you don't. Either you want what God has for you and are willing to do whatever it takes to get it, or you don't. I pray you will accept the criticism from your inner circle and those who love you and use it as an opportunity to grow and birth something new.

I needed to refocus my priorities and hit the reset button. I needed to make sure that nothing was hindering my ability to hear the voice of God—no distractions. I don't know where you are in life; maybe you have a list of dreams or to-do's that need reprioritizing. Maybe your focus has been distorted, hindering your vision and causing you to wander. Will you press in to these next few pages and allow God to refocus your vision and restart a fire in you?

You may still be caught up with trying to figure out what a fire is and how you get one for God. I am so glad you asked. A fire is when you have a passion on the inside for something greater than yourself. When you know Jesus Christ as your Lord and Savior, and when you allow Him to come in and make room in your life for His purposes, you can't help but get a passion and fire for Him. Why would you even want a fire? Simple. So you can be fueled to fulfill the destiny He has specifically for you. Without the fuel or the fire, you won't embrace your *Training Ground*. Fire brings revival. Fire brings refinement. Fire brings the fuel to run.

INVITE THE FIRE

"Our God is a consuming fire" (Hebrews 12:29). God Himself is a Fire that gives passion and fuel to His desires. When we invite Jesus into our hearts and become Christ-followers, we automatically have access to Him and His fire inside us. He begins a work in us to remove those things that are not of Him and make us more into His image, to display His character, but this, too, is a process. We do that by spending time with the Lord and His *Word*. If you want to know the mind of God and what He has to say about you and your situation, then you have to go to the Source. You have to read His Word. You also need *worship* because the atmosphere around you is important. Have you ever poured lighter fluid on wood and then tried to light it? It lights much easier than if you tried to light the wood without it. Worship does that for us, too. It sets the atmosphere that makes it easier to press in to hear God.

Gather your items—your Bible (paper or electronic) and your music (or just a song in your heart)—and go somewhere quiet. I prefer my office or outside on the porch. Wherever your spot is with no distractions, get there. Go ahead, I will wait.

Okay, are you there?

Good. Me, too.

Now turn on your worship music and just sit for a minute. Breathe in. Breathe out. Feel your shoulders start to relax, then sing along with the music, listening to the words. Sing that song to Jesus Himself and tell Him how good He is. Thank Him for all He has done for you and ask Him to prepare your heart to receive what He has to say. Turn your focus to what God is saying to you and write it down as the Holy Spirit gently speaks to your heart and reveals His desires to you. Now turn in your Bible with me to Psalm 37:4. (When you are doing this on your own, you can choose any Scripture you desire.) Are you there? Good.

Delight yourself in the LORD, and he will give you the desires of your heart.

—Psalm 37:4

When you spend time with the Lord and seek His way for your life, His desires and plans for you become your desires. Fire refines your desires until they align with God's desires. This is the fuel you will need to run the race God has given you. This is the fuel you will need as you embrace your *Training Ground*. If you need a refocus, this will reignite the flame. If you are new to this, I pray you will begin to develop a passion for the dream and destiny God has planned for you. A fresh desire to do things maybe you wouldn't have desired to do in the past, or even thought of doing, will be stirred up on the inside. A hunger will rise up in you to spend time with the Lord because He desires to spend time with you. When God's desire becomes your desire, you get passion. And passion will lead you to your purpose. When passion meets purpose, you maximize your potential, and purpose meets destiny, allowing you to run the race God has for you. I promise that when you seek God's direction for your life, you will find the passion and purpose for which you were created, to live a fulfilled life.

Now that we know how to invite God to start the fire, how do we keep it burning? How do we keep our focus? How do not burn out or burn up? These are all questions we ask ourselves at one point or another in our faith walk.

KEEP THE FIRE BURNING

How else do you keep a fire burning? You add more wood.

FEED THE FLAMES

Continue to read, worship, and give thanks. Growing in your relationship with Christ as well as running your race is a continual process. Training is a continual process, with every new level in your purpose. We have to continue to worship and give thanks for what He is doing in our lives and is continuing to do. One of my favorite Scriptures is this:

> But his delight is in the law of the LORD,
>   and on his law he meditates day and night.
>
> He is like a tree
>   planted by streams of water
> that yields its fruit in its season,
>   and its leaf does not wither.
> In all that he does, he prospers.
>
> —Psalm 1:2–3

I prefer to say it this way: "*My* delight is in the law of the Lord, and on *His Word*, I meditate day and night. *I am* like a tree planted by streams of water, whose leaves do not wither but bears fruit in season and *whatever I do prospers!*" You can say it however you want to, but I found that the more personal

I can make His Word to me, the more my fire burns. I can see the benefits to reading His Word in my life.

The Bible tells us in Romans 10:17 that "faith comes from hearing, and hearing through the Word of Christ." According to Psalm 1:2–3, I am full of life, healed and whole. I am fruitful and not barren. I have what I need because God provides for me. I am blessed and prosperous with an abundance of more than enough (Shannon's version). You are full of life, healed and whole. You are fruitful and not barren. You have everything you need because God provides for you. You are blessed with more than enough, and whatever you put your hands to prospers.

You may say, *That's great, Shannon, but I really don't feel like it. I just plain don't feel like worshiping, I don't feel like reading the Bible, and I don't feel like getting up early or making time for the things of God.* Hey, I get it. I have been there, spent the night, and bought the T-shirt. Pastor Steven Furtick said it best: "Passion is not a feeling; it is an action. You have to practice your passion."[1] Practice makes perfect, but let's face it, practice usually isn't fun. There are some days when you have a great practice and some days when practice is brutal.

Many times, I do not want to get up and run to train for the race. Many times I do not want to practice running. If you have ever been to southeast Texas, the weather changes every thirty seconds. It's humid, rainy, and what I call "Africa hot" in the summertime, not to mention when it's cold, it's a wet cold with "gale-force winds." Oh yes, and let's not forget about the mosquitoes!

There are many times when I do not *feel* like running, but then I am reminded that every athlete disciplines himself in both his body and his mind in order to run. So, if I can be so diligent to train and practice running physically for a natural race, how much more diligent should I be to train and practice for my spiritual race? The race God designed just for me. The race for which He gave His life so that I could run. What you feed grows—so feed the flames.

ILLUMINATE

The definition of *illuminate* means "to brighten with light" or "to be enlightened spiritually."[2] Much like fire is used to refine silver and gold to rid them of impurities in order to shine brightly, so are you. The more time you spend with Jesus and getting to know Him through His Word, the more you will be refined. As you are refined, you will illuminate brighter and brighter. You will begin to live like Him, and others will take notice. When you are visibly bright for Jesus, your fire will be displayed by your actions, words, and character. When we become Christ followers, we are not supposed to be undercover Christians. This is not some secret-agent, covert operation of a race we are trying to run. We are to become more like Him. We are to live for Him. Openly. Unashamed, every day of the week—not just on Sundays, when we go to church.

> *No one lights a lamp and then puts it under a basket.*
> *Instead, a lamp is placed on a stand, where it gives*
> *light to everyone in the house. In the same way,*

let your good deeds shine out for all to see, so that
everyone will praise your heavenly Father.

—Matthew 5:15–16 NLT

A good way to know whether your fire is illuminating for Jesus is whether or not you are producing fruit in your life and people are seeing it. The Bible tells us that we will know true disciples by their fruit. You can't follow Jesus and not produce fruit; that would be a contradiction to His Word, and we already know that the Word will never contradict itself. That's also how you know if what you are hearing is the truth. Is what you are hearing lining up with God's Word? Think of it this way: If I give you a lemon and it's yellow, it looks like a lemon, and it smells like lemon, you don't have to go ask someone if it's a lemon. You already know. The same goes for us as Christians. If we are living our lives according to God's standard and putting Him first, we will produce fruit, and people won't look at us and wonder whether we are Christians; they will know by the fruit produced in our lives.

> *But the fruit of the Spirit is love, joy, peace, patience,*
> *kindness, goodness, faithfulness, gentleness, self-con-*
> *trol; against such things there is no law.*
>
> —Galatians 5:22–23

When you illuminate, you shine so bright for Jesus that others will know you are a Christ-follower—by the way you carry yourself, act, speak, and treat others. If others have to ask whether you are a Christian, that should be a clue that you are not illuminating brightly, that either your fire is not lit or it is going dim. If you are not shining as brightly as you want to, don't beat yourself up. There is no condemnation for those who are in Christ Jesus (Romans 8:1). Refining is a process. Bearing fruit takes time. Refining takes time. Refining is *Training Ground*. Gather your wood and feed the flame.

RADIATE

To *radiate* means to "send out" or to "proceed in a direct line toward or from a center."[3] Have you ever experienced pain that started in one place and then radiated to another place in your body? To *radiate* is described as "spreading." When you feed your flames and illuminate, you will automatically radiate out to others. This isn't something for which you have to strive. When others see the fruit you are producing, they will begin to want what you have. The fire you have will spread to others: It will spread in your homes, to your brothers and sisters, to your aunts and uncles, to your friends, your boss, your coworkers, and even other people in your church.

Think about it this way: When was the last time you were around someone encouraging, and how did that make you feel? Good, right? When was the last time you were around a "Negative Nelly" who was pessimistic and whose attitude was terrible? How did that make you feel? Exhausted? Drained and negative yourself, right? Which of these people do you want to be around the most? Hopefully it is the person with the encouraging, positive, uplifting attitude!

You have the power and authority to take control of your atmosphere and illuminate for Jesus so you spread His goodness and joy and radiate it out to others. When you are running the race designed for you, others will see you training, see you running, and begin to run with you.—simply because you make it look so bright! Training for and completing my first marathon woke up a desire in a dear friend of mine. Doctors told her she would never be able to run and that she should just succumb to riding a bike. After encouragement, belief, and training, she, too, is training for her first half marathon (13.1 miles). Praise God! That's what radiating does. It causes others to get excited, encouraged, and equipped to run, too!

EXPECT

Do you really expect God to move on your behalf? Do you really expect Him to do miracles in your life? Do you really expect to hear from God and receive a revelation through His Word? I didn't think so. Most people think that actually hearing from God, actually experiencing answered prayer and miracles, is for "other" people. Many don't think they are "good enough," "worthy enough," "righteous enough," or sadly, "suffering enough" to hear God speak or see Him move in their lives. But guess what? He wants to speak to you. He desires to fellowship with you. God is not too busy for you. That's right, *you*. You, the one holding this book right now. He wants you to lean into Him and feed the flame!

*Now to him who is able to do far more abundantly
than all that we ask or think, according to the power
at work within us.*

—Ephesians 3:20

When you expect God to speak to you about your situation, when you expect Him to respond to your cry and move on your behalf, He will. God wants you to expect Him to do what He said He would do. He is more than able to do exceedingly, abundantly, more than you could ever imagine, according to the power that works *in you*. This means He will use you as a means for an answered prayer, a miracle, and a vessel. His power will work through you if you expect it and believe it. God wants to exceed your expectations and "wow" you! As you feed your flame, as you worship, and as you pray, expect God to respond. Expect God to move on your behalf. Expect God to direct you toward your destiny.

Let's recap. How do we keep the fire burning? *F.I.R.E.:* Feed the Flame, Illuminate, Radiate, and Expect!

- F: Feed the Flame
- I: Illuminate
- R: Radiate
- E: Expect

I am so thankful for Mile 2. I am so thankful for being able to refocus and learning to hear again. I am thankful for the rekindling of the flames and for the re-ignition of my passion for the race that I have been called to run, both physically and spiritually. I am so grateful for pastors who recognize that we are human, encourage us, see us at our best and at our worst and still love us. I pray that the newly lit fire inside you will fuel you to run the race God has marked out for you. Whether you are called to be homemaker, a teacher, a pastor, a doctor, or a lawyer, do it for His glory. Whatever God has called you to do in this season, make the most of it and run for His glory. Now that you have fuel, let's keep running!

TRAINING QUESTIONS

1. Do you have a relationship with Jesus?

2. Do you believe God has a plan and purpose for your life?

3. What priorities need to be adjusted in your life in this season?

4. Where do you need to refocus your attention?

MILE 3

WHO AM I?

Who am I? To whom do I belong? Before you get too far into your race of life, you need to know who you are. Identity seems to be a hot topic in society today, but there, it is rooted in confusion. Many individuals are vying for attention but aren't sure how to obtain it. When people don't know their worth and the value they hold, attention-seeking begins with changing who they are—right down to gender transformation. Knowing who you are is vital to your future success and destiny.

All too often, when I ask people who they are, people tend to respond with what they do, a job title such as:

- I am a nurse.
- I am a doctor.
- I am a teacher.
- I am a housekeeper.
- I am a stay-at-home mom.
- I am an entrepreneur.
- I am a runner.

That may be what you *do*, but that is not who you *are*. You cannot identify yourself with temporary job titles—because what happens when you lose the job? Strip away the professional license: Who do you become? The business fails, and you close the doors: Who are you now? When you retire, who are you? When you identify yourself with tangible and seasonal titles, because everything has an expiration date, you will eventually lose who you are, and confusion sets in. Your identity cannot be tied to a season. Your identity must be rooted in truth, immovable regardless of the job.

When you know who you are and your identity does not change when the seasons do, you fortify your character and propel yourself into purpose. Running this race of life will require that you know who you are and to Whom you belong. Your identity must be forged in something greater than yourself, something greater than temporal sustenance.

If you do not know who you are, the culture and society of the world today will be glad to conform you to the world's definition of identity through lies and deception. This could include, for example, children and adults deciding they prefer to identify as a different gender than what they were born with, or even still, identify themselves as an animal or use non-gendered language to describe their gender. These are all lies and deception from Satan himself.

In order to know who you are, you must first know Who created you and to Whom you belong.

You were created by God—the One True God—and you ultimately belong to Him.

For you formed my inward parts;

you knitted me together in my mother's womb.

—Psalm 139:13

As you pose the question, "Who am I?" let me tell you about the *I AM.*

"God said to Moses, 'I AM WHO I AM'" (Exodus 3:14). When Moses asked God who He was, the name revealed was "I AM." God's name is "I AM."

Before God revealed Himself as the "I AM," Moses' identity was in question from his birth. Born as a Hebrew slave yet raised by the Egyptians, Moses was educated as an Egyptian, clothed as an Egyptian, and reaped the benefits in the palace as an Egyptian. This went on until the moment he realized deep down who he was beneath the fake identity society had created for him. He witnessed one of his own kind, a Hebrew slave, being beaten by what he himself had become—an Egyptian. Moses snapped under the weight of the love for his people and the mask that had become natural to him. He committed murder. When the Egyptians—the ones who had raised him, clothed him, and fed him—found out what he had done, they turned on him. After all, he had never really been one of them. Moses ran in fear for his life.

It would be roughly forty years before God would speak to him in the dry place and introduce Himself as the "I AM," forty years of running and questioning, *Who am I?* By now, Moses was eighty years old, still wondering, *Who am I?* Even after Moses experienced the redemptive power of God through a burning bush and was directed to lead God's people out of slavery, he still questioned who he was. In fact, he tried to tell God, "Um, I think You have the wrong person." He made up excuses about being slow in speech, not eloquent enough, and even begged, "Please send someone else" (Exodus 4:13).

News flash: God doesn't make mistakes. He doesn't change His mind, and He doesn't change His plans. God is pretty sure of Himself and confident in whom He has chosen. He knows exactly who He is, whom He has called, and for what purpose. Moses would eventually come to grips with who the I AM was and who *he himself was*, to fulfill His purpose. Moses eventually realized that the I AM was whatever he needed Him to be. That's right: God is whatever you need Him to be. He is the I AM, the preface before whatever you need Him to be!

God chose you, just like He chose Moses. God is confident in you, just like He was confident in Moses. God created you for His pleasure, for His glory. God planned you. You were not created by accident, nor by happenstance. Regardless of how your natural parents brought you into the world, or what society has tried to conform you to, He knew you before He formed you in your mother's womb (Jeremiah 1:5). Who does your Creator say you are? That is the real identity question. Too often, we are asking the question "Who am I?" of the wrong people. If you want to know who you are, you have to know the answer to who I AM. You have to go to the One who created you.—to the source, to the I AM.

> *So, God created man in his own image,*
> *in the image of God he created him;*

male and female he created them.

—Genesis 1:27

Who does your Creator say you are? You have been created in the image of the I AM. You reflect your heavenly Father. Let me give you a few pearls of wisdom that will bring clarity to the I AM who created you and the image He sees within you. I have two children—eight and eleven years old—who both attend public school. From the time I started taking them to school, I would make them speak what we call in our home, "I AM" statements. Before my children get out of the car in the mornings, they must tell me who they are in Christ. Our conversations go something like this:

Mom: *Who are you?*

Child: *Oh, Mom, do I have to???*

Mom: *Yes! It's not an option. It's my job to teach you who God says you are, or you will get to school and other kids will try to tell you who you are not. If you don't know the truth, you will believe the lie. Now, who are you?*

Child: *"I AM a child of God. I AM free from sickness, poverty, lack, and every kind of bondage and strong-hold. I AM wise and intelligent. I AM creative. I AM exquisite. I AM a daughter of the King, and I have the full armor of God on, ready to face the day.*

Now, that's a kid who knows *"who I am in the I AM."*

Full disclosure: I do have to pull it out of them sometimes. Because my kids have rehearsed their I AM statements so many times and committed them to memory, they will try to speed through the statements to hurry up and finish. Pulling the reins to slow their speech and cause them to really think about who God says they are is a work in progress. Why am I telling you this? Because I want you to know who you are in Christ, so that you can say confidently, "I know who I am in the I AM"—and own it, even when it's rehearsed. It's on the tough days that you will seek to recall it, and if you already have it buried deep in your soul, it will bubble to the top when you need it the most.

I've included some declarations here for you to speak out loud using the preface "I AM":

- Created in His image
- A son and/or daughter of the King
- A royal priesthood

And then, of course, all the added benefits that come with royalty. I AM:

- Forgiven
- Redeemed

- Blessed
- Highly favored
- Healed
- Whole
- God's masterpiece
- Wise
- Intelligent
- Creative
- Unique
- Gifted
- Seated in heavenly places
- The apple of my Father's eye
- And so much more!

When you know who you are and to Whom you belong, you won't believe the lies of the world. God does not use your past or the mistakes you have made to define you. He sets your identity up front, but too often, we let our jobs identify us. We allow people to define us, and we allow our past to dictate our future. We end up saying things like, "I AM tired; I AM useless; I AM lonely; I AM fat; I AM too short... or too tall." Here's a revelation: Every time you preface an adjective used to describe yourself, you are saying God's name up front. God is *not* tired. God is *not* useless. God is *not* lonely. God is *not* fat, too short, or too tall. God is the I AM. He is whatever you need Him to be in that moment, and because He is in you and you are in Him, you can be confident in who you are.

Ultimately God has always had you in mind. Jesus Himself had you in mind when He was tested by Satan in the wilderness for forty days. On the night before Jesus was to be crucified, He went to the garden to pray. We get a glimpse of this conversation between the Son and the Father as Jesus poured His heart out for you. Jesus didn't pray for Himself; He prayed for you—that you would become one with Him. He had you in mind when He prayed in the Garden of Gethsemane. He had you in mind when He went to the cross for you.

> *I do not pray for these alone [it is not for their sake only that I make this request], but also for [all] those who [will ever] believe and trust in Me through their message, that they all may be one; just as You, Father, are in Me and I in You, that they also may be one in Us, so that the world may believe [without any doubt] that You sent Me.*
>
> —John 17:20–23 AMP

To run this race of life, we have to know who we are. Who are you, really? My prayer for you is that you would let go of what you identify yourself with currently and look to the I AM who defines you, the I AM who defines who you are. If you will embrace the truths of who God says you are, you will fulfill your purpose. If you embrace your identity as a child of the King, you can reap the benefits of a Kingdom inheritance. The question "Who am I?" must be rooted in "who I AM." Let go of the past and what you used to define yourself with, and embrace your newfound identity in Christ. You are in the Father, and the Father is in you; the great I AM lives in you. Say this with me out loud: "I know who I am in the I AM!"

TRAINING QUESTIONS

1. What lies of the enemy have you believed about yourself?

2. What have you allowed to define you?

3. With which I AM statement do you resonate the most?

4. How can you identify yourself by who God says you are?

MILE 4

BUILDING CHARACTER

Believe it or not, running builds our character. Running teaches us to endure and persevere through the trials that create mental toughness. Conquering the race in your mind first allows you to create the mental toughness you need to physically forge ahead. Much like I asked you in the identity question—Who are you?—I ask you the same question, but from a different point of view: Who are you when no one is watching? What do people think of when they hear your name? What descriptive words come to mind? Are they words like *excellence*, *loyal*, or *honest*, or are the words a little less flattering, like *wishy-washy*, *dramatic*, or *dishonest*?

Early in my faith journey, my pastor shared with me these words of wisdom: "Your gift will take you there, but character will keep you there." He meant that I could be great at my talent, gift, or skill, so much so that I could climb to the top very quickly. I could be the best communicator in the room. I could be the best salesperson in the room, but if my character did not align with my actions, I would lose credibility, respect, and eventually my post. In other words, he recognized the gift

God had placed in me and wanted to make sure that once I got to where God had called me, I would have the character in place to sustain me. I want that for you, too. God gives us the grace we need for the gift, and the gift will manifest itself. Sometimes others will see the gift in you and elevate you through promotion and platforms, but if your character has not developed in sync with your gift, it could cause delays, or worse, destruction. It takes time to build character, but mere seconds to collapse it. One lapse in judgment on public display can collapse your entire character and reputation.

Your character is what you communicate to others through your actions. Do you operate in integrity? Do you give generously with no strings attached? Do you do things with excellence? Do you keep your commitments and follow through?

How about I go a step further? This might step on your toes, but please don't turn a deaf ear. What do you post on social media? What you post on social media creates a brand for your life! If you vent on social media, you create a brand of drama for yourself. If you post pictures of your body that should only be seen by your spouse, you create a brand of low self-worth and attention-seeking for yourself. In case you didn't know, 55 percent of what people see is what you communicate.[4] If you want to create a brand that is going to attract a healthy business, a healthy lifestyle, and the right people who can help propel you into your purpose, you must be mindful of what you post and the character you are forming. First impressions are often thought of as the impression you make when you meet someone for the first time. The truth is, in this era of social media and the internet, you make a first impression before you ever open your mouth to speak, or before you ever physically meet someone.

It is much easier to make a great first impression when you live what you represent. Perception is everything. Character is not built in a day. Your character is built over time, tested and proved. Character is lining up your actions with your words, living what you believe. Character is living what you represent. This bears repeating: When you live what you represent, it's much easier to make a great first impression.

Developing your character is rooted in the decisions you make. We make decisions every day. We decide what clothes we will wear. We decide whether we will wear black socks or white socks, yet those aren't the decisions that will determine our destiny. Character-development decisions will determine how far you will go toward reaching your destiny.

I will never forget the first time my pastor invited me to speak on a Sunday morning. It was a *kairos* moment for me: *a moment in time when the conditions were right for a crucial action.*[5] *Kairos* moments are God's setup opportunities meant to shift us into our purpose. The decision to say "yes" was a shift toward my destiny and my ultimate calling. The decision to say "yes" was a piece of the puzzle for the greater vision. Our church was in the middle of a series called "Destiny Decisions." The word that God would download to me was one I was walking out and still am, as it is *training ground.* Would you allow me to share with you a few of the nuggets from my very first Sunday sermon? I truly believe that if you apply them, they will build your character and help to prepare you for your purpose. Let's take a look at them here:

DESTINY DECISIONS REQUIRE YOU TO S.H.I.F.T.

S: SELF-DISCIPLINE

Now all discipline seems to be painful at the time, yet later it will produce a transformation of character, bringing a harvest of righteousness and peace to those who yield to it.

—Hebrews 12:11 TPT

We will discuss more about self-discipline throughout the layers of this book, as process has everything to do with disciplining yourself to run the race God has for you. For now, self-discipline is required in how you decide to commit to your growth and character-development process. You decide what you will and will not tolerate from yourself and others. You decide how far you will go before your integrity is called into question. You decide what commitments you will keep to develop your character. Regardless of whether or not you feel like it, you choose to remain disciplined so your character will be transformed and you will become who God has called you to be. Being disciplined includes being honest with yourself and where you currently are so you can make the adjustments. Rather than casting a wide net of self-discipline, get specific on what area in which you wish to be more disciplined. For example, if you desire to lead and influence others, then be disciplined in your personal growth of leadership and be on time. If you want to retire early, then be disciplined in saving

58

and increase your stewardship. Self-discipline means doing the small things consistently, regardless of whether or not you *feel* like it.

H: HUMILITY

But he gives more grace. Therefore it says, "God opposes the proud but gives grace to the humble."

—James 4:6

As part of your training, you have to be humble enough to admit the power doesn't come from you, but from God working through you. Humility opens the door for grace to operate in your gift.

As we shift into character development, I want to draw your attention to David as a youth.

And Jesse said to David his son, "Take for your brothers an ephah of this parched grain, and these ten loaves, and carry them quickly to the camp to your brothers. Also take these ten cheeses to the commander of their thousand. See if your brothers are well, and bring some token from them." Now Saul and they and all the men of Israel were in the Valley of Elah, fighting with the Philistines. And David rose early in the morning and left the sheep with a keeper and took the provisions and went, as Jesse had commanded

59

him. And he came to the encampment as the host was going out to the battle line, shouting the war cry.

—1 Samuel 17:17–20

David had been anointed king several chapters before, yet he was obedient to the role of a shepherd. David had been told his future would be that of a leader over an entire nation, yet the task he was being asked to carry out did not seem like it fit his calling. Shortly after being anointed to be the next king of Israel, he was ordered by his own father to take lunch to his brothers who were on the battle lines.

David could have let pride get the best of him and say, "Don't you know who I am? Don't you know what anointing I carry? Get someone else to carry the lunch." But not David; that mentality was nowhere to be found.

Instead, David acted with such humility and obedience that the power of God and the grace of God rested on him—so much so that this one mundane task set David up to fulfill a purpose, slay Goliath, and step into his calling to become the king of Israel.

I: INFORMED

David asked the men standing near him, "What will be done for the man who kills this Philistine and removes this disgrace from Israel? Who is this

uncircumcised Philistine that he should defy the
armies of the living God?"

—1 Samuel 17:26 NIV

Get informed before making any decisions regarding your purpose and destiny. When we get informed, we ask questions. Too often we are asking the wrong question to the wrong people. We see David attempt to get informed by asking the question, "What will be done for the man who kills the Philistine?"

He gets informed. Then he was met with opposition. His own brothers, the ones to whom he had brought lunch, despised his efforts to get informed. Jealousy was seeping in.

When Eliab, David's oldest brother, heard him
speaking with the men, he burned with anger at him
and asked, "Why have you come down here? And with
whom did you leave those few sheep in the wilderness?
I know how conceited you are and how wicked your
heart is; you came down only to watch the battle."

—1 Samuel 17:28 NIV

Anytime you get informed, you will be met with a crowd that opposes you. You cannot let that opposition deter you from getting informed. In today's society, as Christians and the Church, we must be informed—informed on what the political views are, informed on the landscape of our nation, informed on governmental decisions. When you're not informed, you won't speak up. When you're not informed, you will conform. You must know what the enemy's strategy is so you can combat it with the truth. When you are not informed, you will support the wrong movement. Get informed with the truth before you decide to invest, move, vote, or support. What you permit, you promote; and what you support, you are investing in. If you make ill-informed decisions and support what goes against what you stand for, the perception of your decisions will be a detriment to your character and reputation.

F: FAITH

Now faith is the assurance of things hoped for, the conviction of things not seen.

—Hebrews 11:1

David had what I call unshakeable faith.

And David said to Saul, "Let no man's heart fail because of him. Your servant will go and fight with this Philistine.

—1 Samuel 17:32

This kind of faith will cause you to:

- Step out of your comfort zone and into the purpose God has for you.
- Win the battle against the enemy.

- Carry out the calling God has placed in you.
- Grow from faith to faith and from glory to glory.

Faith is what activates God to move on your behalf. As Christ-followers fulfilling our purpose, much of what we do is done in faith. The steps we take are in faith.

God will give us visions, pictures, and glimpses of our purpose and destiny to keep us going. He will reveal just enough to keep us stepping in the right direction, and when we are obedient and take steps of faith even when we can't fully see the outcome, we get another step. Faith requires action on our part as we know that "faith apart from works is dead" (James 2:26). When we couple our faith with obedience, we receive God's promises. David had faith that he could defeat his enemy. David had faith that he would carry out his calling to be king over Israel. David had faith to step out of his comfort zone, off the field, and onto the battle lines. There are some decisions we make only by faith.

T: TIME

For everything there is a season, and a time for every matter under heaven.

—Ecclesiastes 3:1

Know that the entire premise of the book is going through a process that takes time. Character development takes time.

The road to your destiny takes time, and in that time, there are different seasons and processes during which learning and development takes place. To everything there is a season. David had been anointed king, but not yet appointed. It took time for David to go from the field to the castle, nearly fifteen years of process and character development before he would begin his reign.

It's important to recognize the season you are in so the strategy for fulfilling your purpose is in alignment with the proper season. Just like there is a spring, a summer, a fall, and a winter in each year, there are the same spiritual seasons in the process of fulfilling your destiny. Just like there is seedtime and harvest for a farmer, there is seedtime and harvest for your own destiny. The time is the waiting season. And time is what we have the most difficulty with in today's society. Time is precious because you cannot save it, nor can you get back. Time is a wonderful thing. Everything is made beautiful in its time (Ecclesiastes 3:11): The time between being anointed and appointed. The time between having the dream and living the dream. The time during which the process takes place to prepare you for the appointment. The time during which the process takes place to prepare you to live the dream. This is where process meets purpose.

At the start of my ministry, I was once told by an elder in our church, "Be ready in season and out." At the time, I didn't know what that meant. It wasn't until after I had endured a few processes and challenges that I began to realize what she was saying. There will be seasons of plenty and abundance, when people are asking you to speak on Sundays or at women's events. When that happens, you will study the Word and write sermons with excitement in your spare time, but when the phone calls quiet down and the season becomes dry and quiet, that doesn't mean you shouldn't stay ready. In a season of quietness and dryness, the flesh may choose to shy away from preparing a message or studying. I mean, why would you prepare a message if you have no one to preach it to? Wrong! That's the season of preparation; that's the time to get ready. You get ready *now* for the *then*. You preach to yourself in the kitchen when no one is listening. You dive deeper into the Word to immerse yourself in His presence. If you are expecting and believing for a season of expansion in your marriage, in your business, or in your ministry, then you had better be willing to go through a season of investment. If you expect a season of harvest, you had better be ready to go through a season of sowing. Seasons take time.

Even though this season may not be what you expected or turn out the way you thought it would, give yourself permission to be present in it. Allow yourself to discern what season you are in so you can then prayerfully consider a strategy to keep running in that season. If you do not discern what season you are in, you will expect a harvest when you have not yet planted. Discerning the season you are in is crucial to your next steps as you run your race, because how you steward this season will determine your next season.

Let's recap. Your character is what will sustain you in your gift and purpose. Integrity is who you are when no one is looking. In order to develop your character, you will need to make intentional decisions that requiring you to *SHIFT* to run the race God has called you to run. Self-discipline, Humility, Information, Faith, and Time are crucial to your character development. Running builds character. Your discipline in conforming to the training plan builds your character. Your humility to be honest with where you are and what you need to run this race of life builds your character. Getting informed to make decisions before you train and before your race day is wise. It takes faith to believe you can make it to the finish line, and it takes time to train. As you continue to experience your identity rooted in Christ coupled with decisions to develop your character, you will SHIFT into your purpose.

TRAINING QUESTIONS

1. What do people think of when they hear your name?

2. How are you currently perceived?

3. Identify gaps in your integrity; list them and make a commitment to close them. You may need to seek out an accountability partner to help you in this area.

4. Write out a plan for your character development in order to SHIFT into your purpose. Consider the following areas, including specific tasks you will do each day in a specific area:

   a. Self-discipline (for example, I will read my Bible for ten minutes every morning)

   b. Humility (for example, I will ask God to search my heart for any areas of pride and write out how I can show humility in those areas)

   c. Information (for example, I will consider any areas in which I need more information in order to make an informed decision)

   d. Faith (for example, I will write out any decisions that are requiring me to move in faith)

   e. Time (for example, I will spend time on my character development this week, if necessary, putting this task on my calendar)

RUN ON PURPOSE

What is my purpose? This is the question we all ask at some point. I have spent the first few chapters laying the groundwork for you.

Trust me, you want to achieve God's purpose for your life, not your own. You cannot fulfill your God-given purpose if it is not aligned with your character and rooted in the I AM.

Much like the pieces of a puzzle, each season serves a purpose. If we steward each season well with purposefulness, then, like puzzle pieces, they all eventually come together to form our destiny. When I think of character-building and fulfilling a purpose, I see them as strides taken in tandem with one another to reach the ultimate destiny. I see it that way because seasons change, and thus the purpose you serve in this season may look different in the next season, and of course, character-building takes time.

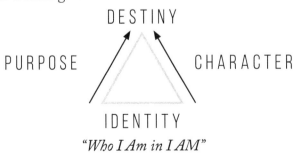

DESTINY

PURPOSE   CHARACTER

IDENTITY
"Who I Am in I AM"

The overarching grand design of becoming a Christ-follower is to lead others to Jesus through the Great Commission, "Go into all the world and proclaim the gospel to the whole creation" (Mark 16:15). That is the same calling for everyone, yet how you do it is contingent on your specific purpose and God-given destiny in life. We are all created by God for a specific purpose. Not everyone's individual purpose is the same. For example, a teacher may fulfill the Great Commission by fulfilling his or her purpose to educate the next generation to be the best version of themselves. A doctor may fulfill his purpose by not only doing his best medically with evidence-based medicine, but by praying with his patients and families with compassion. A pastor may fulfill his calling by planting churches or preparing his Sunday morning sermon. You don't have to be a pastor to fulfill the Great Commission. It is a command we are all given as Christ-followers. How you carry it out should be congruent with your purpose, and the only way people will allow you to influence them in this area is if they see you living it yourself. Therefore, your character must be in alignment with who you say you are.

Outside the call to fulfill the Great Commission, the question I hear the most is this: What is my purpose? Or, How do I find my purpose? Again, all too often we ask this question to the wrong people. If you want to know your purpose, you have to go to the One who designed you. Your Creator placed gifts and talents inside you for a specific purpose. Whenever I am asked this question, I usually answer it with another question: What would you do for the rest of your life, if no one paid you to do it? In other words, what is your passion?

Often our purpose is connected to something about which we are passionate. People often look externally for the answer to finding their purpose, but our passions and purpose are found internally, deeply rooted within. There is an internal fire that is ignited when we think about that which we are passionate about, when we dream about it and expect it. Defining your purpose goes beyond a job title or career.

Maybe your purpose in this season is to impact someone as a first responder by saving someone's life or rescuing someone from a burning building. Maybe your purpose is to provide a genuine smile and greet someone with kindness by fulfilling the role as a greeter in your local church. Purpose goes far beyond a job. Purpose goes far beyond a career. Purpose is innate. Purpose comes from within, and it causes transformation inside others. Purpose leaves an impact; it's more than just your trade.

For fifteen years, I worked in health care, leading and influencing others. In that season, there were character-building moments, moments of humility, and moments of growth. The job served me well. I was able to invest in other leaders' growth and development. I was fortunate enough to add value to others by praying with my team and my patients. My purpose in that season was to glean new leadership skills and learn how to lead and influence others with the truth. Being the chief nursing officer—that was just the title; being a nurse—that was the trade. The purpose was much deeper, and the development of new skill sets and embracing that season is what caused that particular season of investment to push me into a season of expansion.

71

In 2021, I knew God was beginning to shift me into a transition out of health care. Deep down, I know I am called to ministry, and I desired to work for our local church. What I had in mind was that I would work for the church part-time and launch into entrepreneurship as a leadership consultant to make up the salary difference. Through prayer, preparation, and wise counsel, I made the transition. But it didn't quite turn out the way I expected. For other family reasons, which I won't disclose, I didn't go to work for the church; it just wasn't the right time. But God. God blessed my leadership consulting business exponentially, like I had never thought possible. I still serve in our church. I still love my church, and I know God is not finished.

This new season looks different, and it feels different. Even though it didn't turn out like I expected, I am still fulfilling my purpose in this season. I am still investing in people—in particular those closest to me, my husband and children. My purpose in this season is to be present as a wife and mom, not a health care executive. Seasons change. My purpose in this season is to fulfill my calling by reaching the people to whom I have been called in this season. How I treat this season determines the expansion of the next season until the grand design and destiny is reached. This is how you run your race, the race God called you to run.

My personal definition of *purpose* is doing for someone else that which I was created for. Purpose is never just about me; it's always connected to someone else, whether it's in the moment for the here and now or it's for the next generation. Purpose should leave a legacy, whether that's a legacy known all around the world for millions of people or a legacy known for your family and who you are as a parent or grandparent. My desire is to leave a legacy of Jesus. A legacy of integrity. A legacy of prayer. A legacy of blessing and a legacy of generosity.

I want to draw your attention to the verses below:

> *In Him also we have received an inheritance [a destiny—we were claimed by God as His own], having been predestined (chosen, appointed before-hand) according to the purpose of Him who works everything in agreement with the counsel and design of His will.*
>
> —Ephesians 1:11 AMP

You were chosen and given a destiny by your Creator for a purpose, and that is to make an impact for the Kingdom of God. You don't have to be a world-renowned preacher or lead a multimillion-dollar industry or ministry to do that. Your purpose in this season may be to invest time and discipleship in the children with whom you have been gifted. Your purpose may be to pray with your patients in a hospital or clinic. Your purpose may be to lead others in worship to usher them into the presence of God on Sunday mornings at your local church. God has already mapped out the plan He has for you in advance. All you have to do is be obedient and walk in it.

*For we are his workmanship, created in Christ Jesus
for good works, which God prepared beforehand, that
we should walk in them.*

—Ephesians 2:10

It's easy to want to do our own thing, whether that's chase a career, climb the corporate ladder, or satisfy our flesh with material and temporal substitutes. When we do our own thing, we forgo God's plan altogether, or we run so far ahead that we actually get ahead of God. Let me explain. I am a visionary, and seeing the big picture comes easy for me, sometimes to my detriment. I have been known to get so excited about the big picture that I take off running and forget about those who are connected to me. What's wrong with that? Others get left behind, and I get ahead of God. When that happens, it messes things up and causes delays, but when I wait on God and move in step with Him, it's much easier and smoother. It's not as fast as I want it to be, and most often, it's not done in the way I would have done it, but that's the best part. His ways are better than mine, and when I fulfill His plan for my life, His way, it always turns out better, in every season.

When I was in my early teens, I was so on fire for God. I took my first mission trip to Mexico in my youth. I knew then in my heart that I wanted to impact the Kingdom, but I wasn't sure how. During that mission trip, I saw and learned about demonic influences and the healing, miracle-working power of God. When I arrived back home to the States, I couldn't wait to share what I had seen and how I had witnessed God move.

Somehow, though, no one else could relate, and I couldn't understand why.

A cascade of events would happen that would cause me to fall into the wrong crowd. My parents argued a lot while I was growing up, and they eventually stopped going to church, so I thought, *Why should I continue to go to youth group?* My childhood trauma from being sexually abused by a family member was still a wound that hadn't healed, which led to me looking for acceptance in all the wrong places.

I derailed. I forgot about God and the plans He had for me, but somehow His grace still covered me. Even though I forgot about Him, He never stopped pursuing me. I would make it out of high school, graduate from college, and marry an amazing man, eventually becoming a mother of two beautiful children. It wouldn't be for another fifteen years that I would fully recommit my life to Christ and remember His plan for me. You see, God's plan always prevails, despite our detours. He has a way of getting our attention and gently calling us back to Him.

> *Many are the plans in the mind of a man,*
> *but it is the purpose of the LORD that will stand.*
>
> —Proverbs 19:21

If you have been running away from what God has purposed you to do in this season, whether it's out of fear or uncertainty, I want to encourage you to stop running from Him and run to Him instead. Run the race God has called you to run. Is it hard? Yes, sometimes. Is there resistance? Absolutely. Is it worth it? Most definitely. Just like God got my attention and reminded me of who I was and for what I was created, He will do the same for you. Just like He pursued me and covered me, He will pursue and cover you. He has a purpose for your life already prepared; all you have to do is walk in it, or should I say, *run* in it!

TRAINING QUESTIONS

1. What do you believe your purpose is in this season?

2. What stirs a passion inside you?

3. What would you do for the rest of your life if no one paid you to do it?

4. What step of faith can you take today toward that purpose?

BLAZING TRAILS

There is nothing like a cool, crisp 60-degree morning run with the sun shining in a clear sky and minimal winds. Imagine feeling the crisp air with each stride as the warmth of the sun touches your skin.

This particular morning, my family and I were staying in the hill country on about five hundred acres of stunningly beautiful, rocky terrain. Our lifetime friends had recently acquired the land with several dirt trails winding through the cedar trees and wooded areas and multiple ponds, hills, rocks, and valleys. As we took in the beauty, my son and I could not wait to hike the trails and climb the hills—which seemed like mountains in our eyes. We desired the exploration of something new with eager expectation. As we visited with our friends to learn about the property, we learned they had been riding an ATV through the original, existing trails that had grown over, to make them more visible, and that we were free to run on the trails that had been created.

The excitement to run within myself was palpable. The next day, I planned to start at the front entrance of the property and make my way up through the middle, to come out on the west side next to a pond with a huge oak tree. There hung a tattered hammock on a large oak tree on the bank of the pond, which seemed like the perfect resting spot. I would then make my way back when I was ready. It was not a run I wanted to rush through to see how fast I could complete it. It was a run I wanted to savor. A run I wanted to use to rest in the presence of God as I took in the beauty of the landscape. It was a run in which I wanted to notice things, see things. It was a run during which I expected to hear the voice of God.

As I prepared my heart and mind for the run that was set before me on that cool, crisp morning, I set out just as I had planned. I ran on the trails that had been previously marked out for me. Someone had gone before me and forged the trail through that rocky terrain to provide a route for me that was clear of brush and briar patches. This gave me a direction to follow and cleared my path for the run. What I loved about this property was the tranquility of the numerous mountainous hills, valleys, and meadows. As I ran up each hill, I would encourage myself to "take the hill," to "own the hill" with all the effort I could muster. As I would come down the hill on the other side, I would let gravity do its work; this way I did not exert energy, but I actually rested on the way down, all the while being attentive to the terrain so as not to slip and fall on the rocks.

As I ran from the lowest point in the valley to the highest point on the hill, I would have thoughts of slowing down; my legs would remind me of the pain, and the hill would remind me of my lack of oxygen. In fact, an inward battle raged between the voice in my head and the desire in my heart. The voice in my head would say, *Let's stop and slow down and just walk up the hill,* but my heart was saying, *Run faster, take the hill, you can coast on the way down and let gravity do the work.* I had all sorts of emotions and thoughts, but I have to say that as I took each trail, it was exhilarating.

The next day, I had one mile to run according to my training plan. I decided I would invite my ten-year-old daughter to run with me. I knew it would not be fast, but I wanted to involve her and spend time with her more than anything else. Some training days are not about how fast or how far you can go, but rather who is with you in the training. To my surprise, she said yes. You have to know Gracen to know that this was not in her character. Let's just say that if she had her choice, the air-conditioning would take priority, along with television, YouTube, or her sketch pad. Like I had the previous morning, we started at the gated entrance and began to run. As we were winding our way down through the middle meadow to the west side of the property, we crested a massive hill and could see, in all its tranquility, the gorgeous blue water of the pond with the massive oak tree on its bank. Just under the oak tree, the tattered, worn hammock was in view. Our resting place was in sight.

There were many starts and stops during that mile, for after Gracen ran a little, she would then stop a little. Her small legs were not conditioned to run straight through the entire way. I remember encouraging her, saying, "Come on, you're doing great, keep pushing, you're almost there!" I am pretty sure she wanted me to call her dad to pick her up after the first hill, but she did it. She pressed forward and finished the mile through sweat and a few tears. I stayed with her the whole time, even though I could have easily passed her up. I stayed with her and encouraged her, and here is where the spiritual training came for me.

We are not just running for ourselves; we are blazing trails for the next generation. What good is it if I myself make it to the finish line, but I have no one else to whom I can pass the baton? What good is it if I make it to the finish line but have no one else with whom to celebrate? What good is it if I make it to the finish line, but I leave others behind? The race we run is never about us—not really. It's about those coming after us. It's about the legacy we leave, the baton we pass, and the trail we leave to clear the way for others. Much like the trails on the property were marked out before us to show us the right direction, the trails we leave behind spiritually for our kids, grandkids, and others pave the way for the race they are running in life. I don't know about you, but I want to blaze a trail on which my kids and grandkids can run. A trail that will put them on the path the Master has for them. A trail that will point them to the One who will never leave them nor forsake them. I want to blaze a trail for the next generation so that when they run down the hill and hit their lowest point, they will have something they can hold on to that will pull them out. I want to have left a legacy so deep that when my great-grandkids feel like giving up and throwing in the towel, they will know there is a Hope greater than themselves. That is why I wrote this book—to give that same Hope to you. I want you to know there is something greater in store for you. There is a trail cut out by the Master just for you, and His trail is so much better than we could ever cut out for ourselves.

Earlier in chapter 1, I told you I did not like running as a kid and that I had a story for you. Here it is. My dad was bent on teaching me self-discipline and endurance in my youth. He required me to participate in two things growing up: karate and track. There was no option. Karate, he said, would teach me discipline, and track would teach me endurance. I didn't mind karate—it was an outlet for me—but at some point, I outgrew it and lost interest. Running, though? I hated running. I was slow, so my only option was long distance.

I will never forget my first track meet. I was on my sixth and final lap, thank God, because I was the only one left still running. I remember feeling so much pain in my legs, my arms were heavy, and I wanted to quit. I am pretty sure I was crying and whining all the way to the finish line. But the entire time, I could see my dad and a huge smile on his face. His voice was encouraging me with every lap, "You can do it! Come on, you're almost there!" I eventually finished the race—and a few more after that.

I did not understand this lesson of endurance my dad was trying to teach me until I was in my thirties. He wasn't trying to teach me how to have natural endurance; he was trying to teach me how to have endurance *in life*. He knew that in life I would face challenges and obstacles that would require me to keep pressing on and not quit. He knew the mental toughness that would be required of me in this race of life. He knew the resilience it would require to keep going even after I was knocked down. Life is not easy, and many times, each of us wants to quit. We want to stop sometimes before we even start.

I don't know where you are as you're reading this book. You may be on what you think is your last lap; maybe you are just a quarter of mile in or on mile thirty; but don't quit. Push through the pain, push through the heaviness, and push through the tightness in your chest, because running is 90 percent mental and 10 percent physical. If you can win the race in your mind, you can win it everywhere else.

After I had finished the three-mile run on the trail and the one-mile jog with Gracen, I took an aerial-view photo in Google Maps of our location and sent it to my dad, who was back at home battling COVID-19. His text message came back to me: *I decree I will be in shape to run right alongside with you before long, in Jesus' name.* He was fighting for his own endurance in this journey of life; he was fighting for endurance to breathe. He was fighting to push forward with endurance to run the race God had called him to run. I can give you a praise report that we have enjoyed a run together since, and for that I am grateful. Hallelujah!

I have painted the picture for you of three generations of runners who are passing the Kingdom baton of endurance. My question for you now is this: To whom are you passing *your* baton? Whom are you teaching now while you still have time? Whom are you mentoring now while you still have breath? Whom are you running with now while you still have energy? I am blessed to tell you that on this run, I experienced Jesus as Jehovah-Rapha (the Lord who heals).[6] He healed this day my dad and a dear family friend of ours from COVID-19. Thank You, Jesus.

There will be times as you run this race of life when you will need endurance. Maybe right now you are on the mountaintop. Maybe you are starting a new job, or you have a new marriage or a new baby on the way, and everything feels pretty good and exciting. Flag this page and hold on to this Scripture for when the time comes, so you will be able to keep pressing forward when you are thrust into your next challenge:

> *Therefore do not throw away your confidence, which has a great reward. For you have need of endurance, so that when you have done the will of God you may receive what is promised.*
>
> —Hebrews 10:35–36

We may start off confident, but halfway through, when the pressure comes, we begin to second-guess ourselves. We wonder if we are worthy enough, qualified enough, strong enough, or just plain good enough. Let me tell you that Jesus is enough, and because He is enough, you are enough. Our work is never in vain. Remember why you do what you do. Remember why you run and for Whom you are running.

This private property where my daughter and I were running together already had trails paved for us before we ever started. Someone had gone before us and blazed a trail so that we would know where to run. As we ended our trip that weekend, my friend left me with these words: "Shannon, when you come back, I will have more trails ready for you." In other words, he was planning on blazing new trails for me. The trail was already marked out for us before we ever started, and new ones get made along the way. The race for you has already been marked out. Your heavenly Father has gone before you and blazed a trail. Today you have a fresh opportunity to run and blaze new trails for the next generation.

TRAINING QUESTIONS

1. What legacy are you leaving behind?

2. What trails are you blazing for the next generation?

3. For whom are you running?

4. Who is running with you?

MILE 7

THE TERRAIN IS DIFFERENT

There is a stark difference between road running and trail running. The terrain is different. In road running, there is often a smooth or flat surface of asphalt beneath your feet, and you likely have a clear view of your route and what is ahead of you. On the other hand, in trail running, the terrain is vastly different. There is rocky terrain, sandy terrain, or uneven terrain, depending on where you are. In trail running, I have to be aware of where my feet are and the ground beneath them. With every step, there is a keen awareness that is needed of where your feet must land. From dealing with big boulders with gravel to slick mud puddles and holes in the ground, your footing must be sure. It makes me think of a Scripture tucked away in Habakkuk 3:19:

> GOD, *the Lord, is my strength; he makes my feet like the deer's; he makes me tread on my high places.*

As you continue this journey to fulfill your purpose, God will take you to new levels and heights. He will enlarge your territory and take your feet to new lands. With each adventure into new territory, there is new terrain, both spiritually and physically. As you experience new territory on your journey, you will experience new battlegrounds. With each expansion, you will require the necessary equipment to handle the changing terrain.

I want to continue to draw on the famous Bible story of David and Goliath, how a teenage boy defeated a nine-foot-tall beast with just a stone and a slingshot. You can find the story in 1 Samuel 17.

The land was vast, filled with hundreds of thousands of people ready for war. The Philistines occupied one hill, while the Israelites encamped on another, leaving a wide valley in the middle, the battleground. The mighty nine-foot-tall beast of a man named Goliath dressed in 150 pounds of armor would come out from his battle line and taunt the Israelites in the valley until they ran away in fear. Meanwhile, a shepherd boy named David had been tending to his father's sheep in the field, alone. After forty long, treacherous days of this taunting, David was instructed to serve by delivering lunch to his brothers, who were on the battlefield. David, with his servant's heart, rose early that morning to fulfill the directive out of obedience to his father; he had no idea of the battle in front of him. As David delivered the lunch, he witnessed the taunting of the enemy in the valley, but he also witnessed the fear deposited in his people, the people he had already been anointed to lead. David spoke up and with confidence assured the king of the defeat of Goliath. Even at face value, the current king tried to discourage David from fighting: "But you are only a boy! This giant has been fighting since his youth." In other words, no one really expected David to win. Yet, all the time David had spent in the field tending to the sheep, he had been training. He had rescued the sheep from the lion and the bear. He had slain animals larger than himself to prepare him for this challenge, to take him to his mountaintop experience. David responded, "I have been training for this." After seeing the confidence exude from the young boy, King Saul attempted to dress David in his own armor to prepare him for battle. But once David was fitted with the oversized, heavy, ill-fitting armor, he realized this was not the suit for him. In fact, David said he was unable to wear it because he had not tested it. In other words, he had not trained with it; therefore, he would not take it into battle. But that with which he had already trained—the smooth stones, a slingshot, and the Lord of Hosts—he would take. With this preparation in mind, David ran to the valley to meet his opponent. Reaching into his shepherd's pouch, he pulled out one smooth stone and slayed the enemy to achieve victory.

While this was new territory for David and a new giant to face, he was equipped with the right armor, that with which he had trained. Much like David trained every day with the same equipment, and refused to wear new, ill-fitting armor that had not yet been tested, you, too, must train with familiar equipment so that when the battle comes, you will be ready. I would like to spend some time briefly examining the spiritual equipment to which you have access as you expand your terrain, defeat your giants, and run your race.

Finally, be strong in the Lord and in the strength of his might. Put on the whole armor of God, that you may be able to stand against the schemes of the devil. For we do not wrestle against flesh and blood, but against the rulers, against the authorities, against the cosmic powers over this present darkness, against the spiritual forces of evil in the heavenly places. Therefore take up the whole armor of God, that you may be able to withstand in the evil day, and having done all, to stand firm. Stand therefore, having fastened on the belt of truth, *and having put on the* breastplate of righteousness, *and, as* shoes for your feet, *having put on the readiness given by the* gospel of peace. *In all circumstances take up the* shield of faith, *with which you can extinguish all the flaming darts of the evil one; and take the* helmet of salvation, *and the* sword of the Spirit, *which is the word of God,* praying *at all times in the Spirit, with all prayer and supplication. To that end, keep alert with all persever-ance, making supplication for all the saints.*

—Ephesians 6:10–18, emphasis mine

The overarching theme in these verses is to give you the spiritual armor with which you need to fight in spiritual warfare to come against the attacks of the enemy as you embark on new spiritual terrain. There are numerous great books and Bible studies that cover this spiritual arsenal in great detail. My intent here is to show you how the equipment you need in a natural race relates to the spiritual equipment you need for your God-given race in life, to reach your destiny, fulfill your purpose, and maximize your potential.

THE BELT OF TRUTH

Stand therefore, having fastened on the belt of truth.

—Ephesians 6:14, emphasis mine

Every runner has a different preference as to how they pack their accessories (phone, water bottle, etc.) while running. I recently ran a race in which many of the runners wore fanny packs buckled around their waists, with water bottles strapped to the sides. I began to think about how that so keenly relates to the belt of truth and the elements we need for this race called life. As you are running, you don't want anything to hinder your ability for swift movement. You don't want distractions, such as ill-fitting clothing or having to carry anything in your hands. You want to be able to move freely, with confidence. God gives us His very own Truth. The Truth of His Word is like a litmus test, helping us to know the difference between the truth and a lie. Part of knowing the truth is knowing what God says about you and your situation. You can wear the truth of God's Word like a garment everywhere you go, so that when you are faced with a lie, you have the truth of God's Word ready to combat it with.

THE BREASTPLATE OF RIGHTEOUSNESS

…and having put on the breastplate of righteousness…

—Ephesians 6:14, emphasis mine

I choose to run with a water-reservoir backpack with straps that buckle around my chest and core. I prefer this method simply because I feel it's sturdier on my core, and I am able to pack all my necessities, including phone, earbud case, and nutrition packs. What does the breastplate cover? Your chest. It is designed to protect your most vital organ: your heart. Soldiers wore breastplates made of metal, bronze, or chain mail, and their belt was attached to the breastplate, so that the tighter the belt, the more secure the breastplate was, and the looser the belt, the looser the breastplate. I don't know about you, but when I'm running, I don't want anything falling off, and certainly if I were going into battle, I would want to make sure everything was high and tight. You may be thinking, *I'm not righteous; you don't know what I have done.* God knows that, which is why He makes you righteous; He has already factored in our humanity. He extends His righteousness to you and wants you to access it and use it to guard your most vital organ: your heart. He gives us the desires of our heart (Psalm 37:4). Your passion and purpose will be embedded in the desires of your heart because His desires will become your desires.

Above all else, guard your heart,
for everything you do flows from it.

—Proverbs 4:23 NIV

As you are training, it is imperative that you protect the dream and race God has given you. What you allow into your heart is what will come out. If you allow doubt and discouragement in, you will be crippled by unbelief and fear. Everything you do stems from what is in your heart. But if you protect your heart and allow faith in, you will move forward in that faith. As part of your training, I encourage you to acquire an inner circle of faith-driven, wise mentors whom you can trust who will be for you and be honest with you even when it's tough. The steps you choose to take and the race you choose to run are directed by what is in your heart, and because of that, I challenge you to guard your heart at all costs.

YOUR SHOES—THE GOSPEL OF PEACE

… and, as shoes for your feet, *having put on the readiness given by the* gospel of peace…

—Ephesians 6:15, emphasis mine

The type of shoes in which you run matters. The type of spiritual shoes you put on your feet matters.

I once had a knee injury that kept me from running for six months. It turned out I was wearing the wrong kind of shoes

95

for the amount and type of running I was doing. After being properly fitted for the right shoe for the type of running in which I was participating, I noticed a huge difference. I felt like I could run like the wind. With each step, it seemed like my shoes had springs that would propel me forward. I had feet like that of a deer. I moved swiftly and assuredly, with peace, knowing my feet would be on a firm foundation and I could move with ease because I was equipped to handle the challenge of the terrain.

When you are properly equipped with the shoes of the Gospel of peace, you can take the new territory to which God is expanding you. The Gospel of peace is the Good News of Jesus Christ. He tells us in His Word that we are to carry the Good News to everyone; that means you are to actively love like Him, live like Him, and share Him with others. He also tells us in His Word, "How beautiful are the feet of those who carry good news" (Isaiah 52:7). Now, it stands to reason that if my feet carry Good News, they should be in good shoes!

Seriously, though, when God calls you to go to new places that your eyes have never seen before, you can handle the terrain of life and the challenges you face because you are equipped for the battle. You have access to God's peace.

The terrain in the spiritual realm is different, and you have to be equipped for it. Roman soldiers wore a special shoe that had spikes on the soles that would dig into the ground to secure their footing and help them remain standing while they fought their enemies. You may be reading this book while in the midst of a battle, you may be attacked from all directions, or maybe you have been facing the same attack for years, and you wonder whether your breakthrough will ever come. I am here to encourage you to dig your heels in and stand firm with unshakeable, unwavering peace, on the truth of God's Word. God knows the end from the beginning, and His plans are good, to give you hope and a future (Jeremiah 29:11). What shoes are you wearing today?

THE SHIELD OF FAITH

In all circumstances take up the shield of faith, *with which you can extinguish all the flaming darts of the evil one.*

—Ephesians 6:16, emphasis mine

For what are you believing God that hasn't happened yet? Is it for your healing, salvation for your spouse, a wayward child to return to home? Faith is believing what you cannot see. Your faith is like a muscle; you work out at the gym to get bigger physical muscles. If you want bigger faith, you also have to work it out. Faith requires action. Having faith doesn't mean you can sit back and do nothing. Faith without works is dead (James 2:26). There are many things you can do to work out your faith, but I want to draw attention to one in particular:

So then faith cometh by hearing, and hearing by the word of God.

—Romans 10:17 KJV

Training Ground | Shannon Haltom

What you listen to matters. What you tell yourself matters. What I have found is that the pace I set for myself in my head is what I will run. The number of miles I tell myself I will complete before I start is what I will finish. I also have to be honest with you and tell you that sometimes starting is the hardest part. Taking a step of faith to start a business is not easy. Taking the step of faith to forgive in order to mend a broken relationship is difficult. Making yourself start is hard, and sometimes finishing is even harder. What I have learned is that on my long runs, I have to encourage myself. I have to choose not to dwell on the negative thoughts that come in that try to cause me to quit. I have to choose to replace that negative thought of quitting with God's Word.

Most runners run with earphones in their ears, and whether it's from their smart watch or their phone, there is some way to pipe music or a podcast into their ears. This is why I choose to start my run with worship or a faith-filled podcast to start by hearing, so I know that by faith, I will finish. As I was training for my first marathon, I immersed myself in Pastor Steven Furtick's YouTube interview of Bishop T.D. Jakes, "The Crushing,"[7] repeatedly. With every run, there was a new revelation of how God is using this run, this training ground, even the book you have in your hands, as pressure and process for who He is creating in me. This is a nice segue into our next piece of armor, which also coincides with hearing: the helmet of salvation.

98

Mile 7: The Terrain Is Different

THE HELMET OF SALVATION

And take the helmet of salvation.

—Ephesians 6:17, emphasis mine

Depending on the weather, runners may choose to wear some sort of head covering. Some may choose to wear a ball cap to prevent a sunburn or to shield the sun from their face. If it's cold, a runner may wear a beanie to keep warm. In the battle sense, soldiers wore helmets to protect their heads from injury. In this race of life and to fulfill your purpose, you will need this piece of armor to protect your mind. The mind is where the spiritual battleground truly is. Have you ever had crazy thoughts come in and you wonder, *Where did that come from?* The mind is powerful. What you choose to dwell on determines your outcome. You have been given the helmet of salvation to guard and protect your mind from negative thoughts, to demolish strongholds, and to break free to run with all authority and grace the race that has been marked out for you.

> *For the weapons of our warfare are not of the flesh but have divine power to destroy strongholds. We destroy arguments and every lofty opinion raised against the knowledge of God, and take every thought captive to obey Christ.*
>
> —2 Corinthians 10:4–5

When you choose to make Jesus Christ your Lord and Savior, you have the gift of salvation, the gift of grace, and the gift of mercy. You become a new creation. You were created in His image and likeness. Here is the caveat, though: We walk around in a "flesh suit," dressed in humanity, so we battle between the spirit man on the inside and our culture on the outside. We battle with what we want versus what we know we need. None of us is perfect. This is part of how we work out our salvation daily, which means that every day we choose on what we will dwell. Every day you must choose to encourage yourself in the Lord, choose to access the equipment you have daily to run the race God has called you to run.

THE SWORD OF THE SPIRIT

…and the sword of the Spirit, *which is the word of God.*

—Ephesians 6:17, emphasis mine

This is the only offensive weapon you have been given in your spiritual arsenal. It is unique because you can use it in advance. You can run the play to get ahead and attack the enemy. In case you are still wondering, there is power in God's Word. The day before I was slated to run my first half marathon, a dear friend of mine prayed for me using the verse Isaiah 40:31. She prayed that I would run and not grow weary, walk and not faint. She knew there would come a time during the race when

I would want to quit, and she was using the sword of the Spirit to combat the negative thoughts and feelings ahead of time.

> *Death and life are in the power of the tongue,*
> *and those who love it will eat its fruits.*
>
> —Proverbs 18:21

The words you choose matter. Oftentimes, our very own words are the hindrance to our blessing and breakthrough. As you find yourself in the process, you must choose to combat the enemy with the sword of the Spirit, the Word of God spoken in faith. A prayer strategy against your enemy is essential, because I can assure you that if you are doing anything for God, the enemy already has a strategy against you. Start praying now in advance to cover and protect your children, and pray for your grandchildren and great-grandchildren who are not yet born. Pray for your spouse on whom you are waiting. Pray for your children's spouse whom they haven't yet met. Wield the sword of the Spirit that you have been given.

PRAYER

> … praying *at all times in the Spirit, with all prayer and supplication. To that end, keep alert with all perseverance, making supplication for all the saints.*
>
> —Ephesians 6:18, emphasis mine

I would be remiss if I did not include the seventh attribute, and the most important, most effective weapon of the whole suit of armor: prayer. There are many Scriptures that come to mind when I think of this piece of armor. There are also many great books on prayer, how to pray, and what Scriptures to use to pray for certain areas of your life, but that is not my purpose here. It really is too much to cover in this short chapter. What I want you to understand is that prayer is the single most effective weapon you have against the enemy. Prayer is much more than a minimized "shot in the dark."

When my youngest was in preschool, I remember being in a hurry to make it to work as I was dropping him off. In my race against the clock, I rushed him toward the door to shoo him in. He turned, looked up at me with his big, blue eyes, and said, "Mom, you didn't pray for me." *Thud.* My heart fell to the pit of my stomach. Time stopped, and so did everything around me as I bent down and prayed over my son—that he would have courage to face his day and be the light of Jesus to everyone he met. Now, if a preschooler knows the importance of prayer, how much more should we as adults with life experience value prayer? Where is our childlike faith?

Prayer is powerful and effective. Prayer is our opportunity to activate God's promises. Prayer is our opportunity to activate heaven to move on our behalf. If prayer didn't work, it wouldn't be in our arsenal. Prayer is our time to fellowship with God and make war on the enemy. When I run, I use that time to fellowship with my heavenly Father and listen intently to hear His distinctive, still, small voice. When you pray, you take spiritual ground in your God-given race. Praying gives you a strategy, a battle plan to combat the enemy.

While the terrain is different, the armor you need is the same, and you will grow into each piece. So, when you are faced with Goliath, you won't have the need for ill-fitting armor that belongs to someone else, but you will have your own suit of armor, given to you by the Lord of Hosts Himself. Suit up, so you stay equipped and ready to take new territory with swift feet like the deer and take leaps of faith, running the race God has given you.

TRAINING QUESTIONS

1. In what valley do you currently find yourself?

2. With what has the enemy been taunting you?

3. What new tools have you learned today that you need to access and with which you need to start training?

4. Make a commitment to start training with your new equipment.

5. For what or whom can you pray in advance?

MILE 8

TRAINING IN THE STORM

On a dark and rainy night, the summer I was sixteen years old, I had stretched the truth to my parents and headed somewhere I had no business going. I picked up a friend and started to drive to a place I shouldn't have gone. As the rain fell harder, it became more and more difficult to see. As I rounded a curve going at a speed I knew was most likely too fast, the car I was driving hydroplaned. I lost control of the vehicle, flipping several times and crashing into a tree.

My friend was able to get out and run to a house to call for help. She walked away that day with a hairline fracture to her arm. As for me, all I could do was think about the wrong I was doing and how much I was going to get into trouble. I was actually thinking, *How am I going to get out of this car and run away?* Reality set in. I was stuck: My legs were pinned under the dash, and my face was pinned to the hood of the car. I could feel the rain drenching me as I heard the constant blaring of the car alarm coupled with the booming thunder. I wasn't going anywhere.

When the ambulance arrived, I was semiconscious. All I could hear was chatter as I phased in and out of consciousness. Then—there it was! I could hear my cell phone begin to ring in the midst of all the chaos. In my mind, I was pleading for someone to answer it; I just knew it would be my parents. I couldn't figure out how to verbalize my request, but it seemed that the first responders weren't the least bit interested in finding the phone—and rightfully so. My well-being was their main concern, and for that I am grateful. Somehow the phone was answered, yet no one said hello. Just as I suspected, it was my mother, and all she could hear were the words, "Get the jaws of life"; "we are going to cut her out"; "put her in a C-collar"; "her legs are still pinned."

Imagine being a parent on the other end of the line and that is all you hear. You think your daughter is supposed to be safe, because she had told you where she was going. You think you know where she is. My mom thought those things. I put her and my dad through pain and trouble that neither needed to go through, but because of their faith and love for me, they were able to endure and show me the same grace that my heavenly Father did. God pulled me through the storm because He had a plan for me. He was going to bless me with kids of my own. I was going to have the opportunity to impact other people for His glory. God used that storm in my life to deliver me from a sequence of bad decisions and place my feet on a level path toward grace.

PEACE

The men had just spent the entire day soaking in the presence of God and listening to the Word being preached. Now the sun had fallen, and the clear evening sky was blanketed with stars. As they looked out from the wooden boat, the sound of gentle waves and the reflection from the water gave no cause for the men not to follow their instructions. Their Commander in Chief had given the order to go to the other side while He rested from a full day of work. As the men were making their journey across the sea, suddenly a storm raged out of nowhere. The wooden craft was being tossed to and fro, with waves crashing in on all sides and clouds of darkness filling the sky. The rain fell so hard it began to distort their vision. Immense anxiety and fear filled the hearts of the men. "Quick, get the Commander! Wake Him from His nap! Does He even care if we drown?" Awakened from His slumber, the Commander in Chief spoke: "Quiet! Be still!" Immediately, the furious squall ceased. The men were shell-shocked at what they had just witnessed, and they began to wonder who was actually in the boat with them.

This is the story we find in Mark 4:35–41. The disciples had been with Jesus, listening to Him preach to crowds all day. The initial anxious response would not be what I would have expected to hear from them after they had been with the Christ all day long. Yet, are we not the same? I think back and wonder how many times I have gone to a women's conference, or even church on Sunday morning, to hear an encouraging message; I leave full and excited, only to be hit with a storm of life and immediately forget what was just spoken to my heart. Perhaps you can relate. How often do we forget that Jesus is with us in the storm? You have the power to go through the storm and the authority to speak to it: "Peace! Be still."

The disciples were on a mission with the Messiah. In fact, there is a greater reason they were in the boat headed to the other side, the foreign side. When the boat docked on dry land, the first thing Jesus did was deliver. He was met by a man who was demon-possessed, given up on by everyone else, cast out to the grave and bound by chains that could not contain him (Mark 5). Jesus was on a mission to heal, deliver, and set free that one man. Now, if Jesus would go through a storm to get to that one man, will He not do the same for you? The Messiah Himself went through a storm and faced adversity to accomplish the assignment set before Him. Who are we to think we will not face the storms of life? What if the disciples had decided not to go through the storm and turn around because of the wind and the waves? That young man would have missed his deliverance. Who might miss out on their breakthrough and freedom because you give up in the middle of the storm?

Sometimes the storms we go through have nothing to do with us, but everything to do with someone else, and their very life may depend on it. You have the opportunity to impact lives and become a part of the transformation and breakthrough. The enemy gives you the storm or adversity often at the start, because he knows what you are capable of, and he knows who else could be set free because of you, and he doesn't want you to finish your assignment.

The good news is that God works all things out for our good. God will use the storm to make you stronger, and He will use the storm to forge character and experience within you, if you go through it His way—by faith. Remember He is in the storm with you. Peace was seen and felt. Peace was in the boat. Peace was with the disciples in the storm; they just didn't realize it. The disciples themselves were running a race with the Messiah, but they didn't realize it. You, too, are running a race called life. You will face storms in life—that is a given— but you get to choose how you will come out of it.

> *When you pass through the waters, I will be with you;*
> *and through the rivers, they shall not overwhelm you;*
> *when you walk through fire you shall not be burned,*
> *and the flame shall not consume you.*
>
> —Isaiah 43:2

God promises to be with you in the storm: not *if* you go through the waters, not *if* you face a storm, but *when* you do. The writer is letting us know ahead of time that we will pass through the waters of this life. But He is with you in your storm. Don't allow the storm to quench your fire for reaching your destiny. Don't allow the storm to quench your passion for the things of God. Don't allow the storm to quench the fire that burns within you. The storm that you are facing right now—whether it's a bad medical report, an affair in a marriage, betrayal by a close friend, a court case where your character is in question, or a lost child—He is with you. He promises the storm will not overtake you or conquer you, but rather, *you* will conquer *it*. Just as He parted the waters for the Israelites as they were escaping slavery from Egypt and allowed them to walk through the river on dry ground, He will do the same for you. You need only to believe and trust Him to do His part.

This particular morning, I set out on a five-mile run in my parents' quiet country neighborhood. The weather seemed a bit humid, but that was normal for Texas. I completed my warmup, then turned on my podcast, set my watch to an outdoor run, and off I went. I remember thinking, *This is a great pace! It is slightly overcast, with a cool breeze and fresh air.* I was basking in God's goodness, thankful for the ability to run. I felt relaxed and settled. But when I rounded the first mile, I was met with a gush of cold, rushing wind, face-on. The leaves were gusting over the road, and then it happened: The bottom fell out. The clouds opened up, and heavy rain began to fall. There were no gradual sprinkles, no warning signs—just rain. I thought to myself, *I'd better pick up the pace!* I kept running, soon drenched from head to toe. (Now let me be clear: There was no lightning. Unfortunately, I have been caught in a thunderstorm with lightning in the past while running. Please use wisdom whenever you are running and call for a pickup if you ever think you could be putting yourself in an unsafe situation.)

As I was closing in on the fifth mile that day, my dad could see me from his front porch, and he began to get worried—and rightfully so. As any parent would, he was worried I would catch a cold from running in the rain, and he was also worried a car wouldn't be able to see me in the rain. What do dads do in that kind of situation? They run after you. Before I had even realized it, Dad was next to me in his vehicle to pick me up. I waved him off, signaling him to let me finish. By this point, I was determined to finish the five miles, even in the rain. My dad discerned my request and stayed in view the rest of the way, watching from a distance, never letting me out of his sight.

The lesson I learned that day was this: Much like my natural father came to my rescue in the storm, so does my heavenly Father. He always keeps us in plain view, never letting us out of His sight. He is with you in the storm, as well. He is within the storm you face, no matter what it is, even if it takes you off guard with no warning signs. He is in the struggle with you. He is in the pain with you. He is in the valley with you. He follows close by and whispers, *Do you trust Me?* Trust that He will see you through the storm. Have faith that you will overcome and get to the mountaintop. Have faith that you will endure the trial to end. Believe that you fight from a stance of victory, not defeat. You will have to choose to be the one who will run, even when the environmental conditions are less than desirable. You have to choose to run even when it's cold and raining, even when you don't feel like it. This is *Training Ground.*

Just like getting caught in a rainstorm while you are running can cause you to want to quit or turn around, remember that someone else is depending on you to get through the storm. Combat the storm with your God-given authority and hold steadfast to your peace. Our King of kings can give you the peace that surpasses all understanding in the middle of the storm, just as He Himself had peace during His own storm. In other words, you can go through the storm and not respond

111

with anxiety or fear, but rather, you can respond with complete faith and peace, trusting that God is with you in the storm. He is going to see you through it to the other side, and He will use the storm to bring about a good thing. He works all things out for our good. He is in the boat with you. As you are training and then running in this race of life, storms will come, and when they do, remember that they won't overtake you. You are strong enough to get through it. You are qualified and capable to complete the assignment on the other side of the storm. Keep running!

TRAINING QUESTIONS

1. What storm are you currently facing?

2. Who stands to benefit when you make it through the storm?

3. What can you do today to speak peace to the storm you are facing?

4. What action of faith do you need to take to get through the storm?

MILE 9

"LORD, HELP MY UNBELIEF"

*Immediately the father of the child cried out and said,
"I believe; help my unbelief!"*

—Mark 9:24

Have you ever wanted to believe for something so badly, but a nagging feeling of doubt or unbelief lurked in the shadows of your prayers? It is not that we don't want to believe, or that we don't believe for others, but we often have a hard time believing for ourselves. The enemy "comes only to steal and kill and destroy" (John 10:10), and he plants seeds of doubt and unbelief in our minds, hoping to rob us from the very blessing and life God came to give us.

The enemy doesn't have to do much to keep us from moving forward in our purpose. He only has to cause us to doubt our ability so that we won't move forward. The enemy wants you to quit before you ever start, and he doesn't have to do anything drastic. He just has to grip you with doubt: Doubt that you will ever make it to your destiny. Doubt that what you have been believing for will ever come to pass. Doubt that you will ever get ahead. Doubt that your past sin can be overcome and that you can have an abundant future. Doubt in yourself and your ability. The enemy will cause you to believe that every setback is your fault and that you are not worthy of moving forward. If he can keep you crippled by thoughts of doubt—or worse, unbelief—you will quit, or not even start.

If you struggle with unbelief or doubt, you are not alone. It's not that I don't believe in the power of God or His manifest presence. It's not that I don't believe God can move in your situation. In fact, I have tons of faith for you—crazy faith! I believe God can and will move mountains for you. But sometimes I doubt *for myself.* Sometimes I have a hard time believing He will come through for me. That is actually crazy because God has been too good for me not to believe in Him. But there are just some things, mold-breaking things, we go through that cause us to question whether we truly believe it for ourselves.

At first, I doubted. What I had been asking God for had yet to come to pass. I was looking at my circumstances, and doubt hung in the shadows and quickly turned to unbelief that I could ever actually be used for God's glory. I was recently speaking with someone whom I hold near and dear to my heart, and as he shared his same struggle, he spoke of it this way. He used the terms *wrestle* and *fight* interchangeably. He wrestled with himself. He referenced the apostle Paul in the book of Philippians:

> *If I am to live in the flesh, that means fruitful labor for me. Yet which I shall choose I cannot tell. I am*

*hard pressed between the two. My desire is to depart
and be with Christ, for that is far better. But to
remain in the flesh is more necessary on your account.*

—Philippians 1:22–24

In other words, there was an internal wrestle, an internal struggle between me, myself, and I. I wrestled with whether or not I was really gifted, called, or even worthy of a blessing. I wrestled with my calling. As my friend and pastor began to share his own struggle, I could relate, and to be honest, it was freeing. It freed me to know I wasn't alone and that there wasn't something drastically wrong with me. These thoughts of doubt and unbelief are nothing but tactics the enemy uses to keep you from completing what you were called to do. As I expressed my own struggle, I was freed in that moment to know that not only was I not alone, but that there was a remedy for the problem.

TAKE GOD AT HIS WORD

My friend and pastor said something along these lines: "Shannon, God's Word is either true or it isn't." So, I am telling you, God's Word is either true or it isn't. It's either all truth or all a lie. I choose to believe it all. That means I have to choose faith over doubt and belief over unbelief.

When we have thoughts of doubt and unbelief that begin to sneak in, we have to choose to win the fight. We win by taking God at His Word. We choose to believe Him versus the thoughts we have. His Word, the Bible, is either all truth for

117

everyone or all lies, meant for no one. I can't believe one Scripture and not the other. I can't believe the Old Testament and not the New Testament. I can't choose to believe in the death and burial, but not the resurrection. For me, it is all or nothing. I choose to believe. In my mind, I have to choose the Scripture that combats the unbelief to win the fight on the inside. I love this Scripture that the apostle Paul wrote in his letter to the Corinthians:

> *For the weapons of our warfare are not of the flesh but have divine power to destroy strongholds. We destroy arguments and every lofty opinion raised against the knowledge of God, and take every thought captive to obey Christ.*
>
> —2 Corinthians 10:4–5

Paul was saying that we have been given the Word of God as a weapon to combat thoughts we know aren't in alignment with God's thoughts or His plan. When doubt sneaks in, we can take the thought of doubt captive and replace it with a thought from God.

For example, I can choose to doubt my healing and instead believe what the medical report says about my health, or I can choose to believe that by "his wounds we are healed" (Isaiah 53:5). I can choose to believe that I suffer from fear, or I can say, "God has not given us a spirit of fear, but of power and of love and of a sound mind" (2 Timothy 1:7 NKJV). I can choose to doubt that my family will ever be saved, or I can choose to believe that my entire household shall be saved (Acts 16:31). I can choose the feeling of defeat, or I can believe that victory is already mine. I can choose to believe that I have "overcome him [the devil] by the blood of the Lamb and by the word of [my] testimony" (Revelation 12:11 NKJV). I choose to win the war inside of me, the one that is battling against "me, myself, and I," by taking God at His Word.

There are days when I don't believe in myself to run. There are days when I have thoughts about being too slow or not good enough. There are days when I think I will never make it to the race. Yet I choose to bring my mind and flesh into submission, to "discipline my body and keep it under control, lest after preaching to others I myself should be disqualified" (1 Corinthians 9:27). I must choose not to dwell on the negative and discouraging thoughts and choose to replace them with thoughts that line up with God's Word. I encourage you to take God at His Word. Purposefully discipline your thoughts and watch what He will do for you. As you run to fulfill your destiny and calling, there are many lies the enemy will use to instill doubt—I know because I have battled them myself. But by exposing the lie, I am hopeful that you will shatter your own unbelief.

I remember the first time I listened to a recording of myself from my first speaking event. I was mortified! I hated the way I sounded, and I thought, *Who would ever want to listen to me and my country accent!* I wanted to check out right then! I began to have crazy thoughts: *People are laughing at me; people think I am just a country bumpkin!* I began to tell myself there was no way I had been created to speak, and there was no way God could

119

use me to reach other people. I would tell myself that no one wanted to hear me. I wasn't good enough.

Isn't it just like the devil to make us feel dirty, ashamed, unqualified, and worthless? But the truth is, I am who God says I am. Say it out loud with me: "I am who God says I am." I had to learn to push past it, take God at His Word, and choose to believe that I am who He says I am and I can do what He says I can do. I had to take Him at His Word that I was called and equipped for a purpose—and so are you. When you know your Creator and what He says about you, you won't fall for the lie.

Listen, have you seen the roster of the disciples Jesus chose? Have you ever done a background check on those guys? Peter had anger and ego issues, Matthew was a tax collector, and Judas sold out Jesus! Have you seen the family tree of our Savior? It is chock-full of imperfect people, including a drunk, a prostitute, an adulterer, a murderer, and more. They would have all come up on the short list had we used the world's standard of being "good enough." The world's standard sends the message that we have to be perfect, make a certain amount of money, have a degree, and know all the right people. But God's standard sends the message that He makes all things new. News flash: There are no perfect people. Everyone used for His greatness has flaws, but our Creator qualifies the called, forgives us of our sins, and transforms us into His likeness. Jesus has already made up His mind about you, and He knows the plans He has for you (Jeremiah 29:11). He knew you before you were even created in your mother's womb (Jeremiah 1:5). He has already deposited within you every gift you were ever going to need to run your race and fulfill your destiny. It is up to you to cultivate them and use them.

Joyce Meyer wrote in her book *The Battlefield of the Mind* that "doubt comes in the forms of thoughts that are in opposition to the Word of God."[8] I knew then that if I gave in to the doubt, I would most likely forfeit my calling. The devil is a liar! I have come too far to turn back now, and I bet you have, too. You are who God says you are; you are predestined, chosen, a royal priesthood. You are more than a conqueror. When you own who you are in Christ, you can shatter your unbelief and advance forward in confidence.

TAKE COURAGE

Encouragement is such a powerful seed. The words we choose to say to ourselves and to others matter.

I recently participated in a workout on Good Friday known in the CrossFit community as the "Passion WOD". It consists of one hundred double-unders, an eight-hundred-meter barbell carry, and one hundred burpees. Each movement held significance. The double-unders were to remind us of the lashings that Jesus received with the cat-of-nine tails, which He took for you and me. The barbell carry was to symbolize Jesus carrying His own cross on which He would be nailed, and the burpees were to represent Him conquering death and rising again.[9]

Prior to the workout, one of our coaches challenged us to complete the entire workout in silence. Now, if you know anything about CrossFit, this community of people is constantly encouraging one another as workouts are completed. To complete this workout in silence was challenging and went against our nature during a normal workout routine. But as we completed the workout, I couldn't help but realize just how important it is that we encourage the body of Christ.

Think about it. Why is it so important that we encourage one another? When you are encouraged, you are inspired, motivated, and energized to keep going. When you are encouraged, you quicken your pace and push through when it gets hard. When you are encouraged, you lift heavier weights and improve your personal best. Jesus wasn't doing a workout for fitness when He went to the cross. He was submitting Himself to the will of the Father so that we could experience eternal life with Him. His entire purpose on earth was to die so that He could conquer the grave for you and me. There was no one cheering Him on to complete His race. There was no one encouraging Him to fulfill His purpose. There was no one on the sidelines cheering Him on, "You can do it, Jesus. Hang in there!" In fact, one of His own disciples would, rather than follow Him to Calvary, stop by the enemy's camp to warm himself and then deny Him not once, but three times.

Now, though, because of God's goodness and love for you and me, His plans for us are good. As we run our race in life and fulfill the purpose God has for us, we want to be supported and encouraged. The truth is, even though God's plan is good, not every day *feels* good. Some days are tough; some *seasons* are tough. If we are honest, there are days when we want to quit and throw in the towel. There are moments when we battle doubt and unbelief. This is why we need encouragement. Our flesh is weak. We are not meant to run this race alone or in our own strength. We were called to encourage each other, to build each other up.

In this race, if you are really running, you require daily encouragement. If you have an inner circle strong enough to encourage you every day, you are blessed. But not many people have that. Because of that, we must learn to encourage ourselves in the Word. You learn to encourage yourself by reading the Word of God. You must remind yourself of His encouraging promises. You must have a "whatever it takes" attitude to persevere and push through. This may mean posting encouraging Scriptures that are easily accessible for you to review when you need them the most. You must decide to set an encouraging atmosphere.

Until you learn to encourage yourself, will you allow me to encourage you today? You don't have to walk this out alone; the Hope of glory lives inside of you. In your weakness, He is strong. You can get through this season of life. You can run your race. You can keep going and experience breakthrough and victory. You can possess your blessing. You can do it! Don't lose heart. Take courage! Remain steadfast! Be strong and courageous, for the Lord Himself is fighting for you! If God is for you, who can be against you? He will never leave you nor forsake you. He is faithful. God is not a man that He should lie. He doesn't change His mind. Do not fear; He will hold you up and perfect all that concerns you. He will supply all your needs according to His riches in glory. He is working on your behalf even when you don't see it. Right now, He is putting in alignment everything you need for your race. He has called you, chosen you, predestined you, and qualified you to fulfill your purpose for His glory.

As you choose to take God at His Word, learn to encourage yourself and take captive every thought to push the doubt out. I encourage you to keep running the race God has set out for you. There will be times when you mess up and miss the mark, but there is grace for that. There will be times when you step out in faith and obedience, unsure of where it will lead you, but there is grace for that, too. This is good training ground for you, training on how to combat doubt. Push back the doubt by taking every thought captive and making it obedient to Christ. Use every weapon in your arsenal to combat the enemy. Your training is ongoing. Training is a process. Let's keep running.

TRAINING QUESTION

1. For what are you believing God that has yet to come to pass?

2. Are you struggling with doubt or unbelief?

3. What lie is the enemy currently telling you?

4. Look up a Scripture that will help you combat the lie and believe God for your miracle.

5. Write out three Scriptures and post them somewhere you will see them every day to encourage yourself.

MILE 10

FUEL

Keeping fuel on your fire is essential to prevent burnout. Even if you think you have half a tank or a reserve, I promise you, you want to stay full at all times. You will feel the effects of a low tank.

I am embarrassed to admit that I am bad about keeping the gas tank in my car full. All too often, I wait until the gas light comes on—and then I check the section on the screen that tells me just how many miles I have left to go before I run out, placing all my faith in its calculation!

When you let your spiritual tank run low and the fuel light comes on, you normally aren't riding on faith to the church house to get refueled. Why is that? Because your faith has been depleted, your energy is zapped, and stress and exhaustion have set in. At this point, you are the most vulnerable to the attacks of the enemy and easily tempted to walk away, backslide, or fall into a pit of despair. This is why it is so important that you stay fueled up and keep your fire burning. Just like the engine in your car requires the proper fuel to maximize your mileage, so does your body require the proper the fuel to run its race.

Before I go any further, let me preface this chapter with the admonition that you should check with your trainer or medical professional to determine the proper nutrition and hydration that is best for you.

HYDRATION

My first half marathon was a trail race, and I was unprepared, to say the least. I didn't realize there was such a vast difference in the aid stations as compared to road racing. I was used to small 5K (3.1-mile) runs with water stations that had tables with cups of water that runners could grab as they ran past. That morning as I arrived, I noticed many people had packed their own water bottles and strapped them to their waists or backs. I had thought the less I carried, the better. I hadn't yet begun to train with a water reservoir backpack, and honestly, I preferred not to have the extra weight to carry. I was anticipating water stations along the way. Now, naturally, I have built up an endurance capacity to go without water for at least the first ten miles; even though that's really not the smart thing to do, under pressure, my body can do it, because I have trained for it. My plan for this race was to take in water at the ten-mile mark and then finish the last 3.1 miles.

Here is what really happened. I started the race, and I passed up the first two aid stations. When I arrived at the ten-mile mark and the last aid station, I asked for water, only to find out it was a cup-less race. In an exasperated and confused tone, I asked, "What does that mean?" I was told I needed to bring my own water bottle to be refilled to minimize litter along the trail. That was definitely key information I had not had prior to the start of the race.

What the aid station *did* seem to have, however, were energy-type, seemingly-carbonated drinks in one-ounce cups. I thought that something would be better than nothing, so I took one, kicked it back, and threw the cup in the trash—only to find out that what I had just swallowed was pickle juice! Things were not going well for me.

What is the main ingredient in pickle juice? Salt. What does salt do? Cause a person to thirst. Needless to say, I finished the last grueling 3.1 miles dehydrated and exhausted, with an unquenchable thirst.

In my research for this book, I found that our body has close to the same percentage of salt as does the ocean. One of the most common salts is sodium chloride (table salt), which makes up about 0.4 percent of our body weight. To put that into context, a person who weighs 110 pounds has approximately 2.5 cups of salt in their body naturally.[10]

Our bodies need salt to function, so—without getting off into a pathophysiology course—our hearts require a certain level of salt to pump effectively.[11] It is no mistake that our Creator made us to need salt to function. The Bible says that we are the "salt of the earth" (Matthew 5:13). Salt has many different purposes: It can be used to add flavor, it promotes healing, and among other things, it causes you to thirst. When you sweat, you lose salt, which is why it is important to replenish your stores. When you have the right amount of salt, you promote healing in your body. When you have the right amount of salt, your heart can pump effectively. When you have the right amount of salt, you have flavor—and people enjoy being around you because of the flavor you bring to the environment.

In the spiritual race we are running for Jesus, if we aren't careful we can become dehydrated; we can lose our saltiness.

Allow me to share with you how and why you should stay hydrated and maintain your salt balance.

LIVING WATER

She was tired and worn, and her past with different men haunted her. She had become numb to the pain and dehydrated without even knowing it. The clock struck noon in the middle of the day as she made her way to the town to draw water from the well, hoping to satisfy a thirst that never seemed to go away. The last thing she needed was to encounter another man—or so she thought. As she let down her pail to draw from the well, she heard a man's voice ask her for a drink of water. As she raised her head and her gaze met His, she knew on the inside something was different about Him, yet it wasn't customary for a Jewish man to speak to a Samaritan woman. "Who am I that You would ask me for a drink?" she said—only to receive the counter-response from a Man she didn't even know, "If you knew the gift of God, and who it is that [asks you for a drink], you would have asked him and he would have given you living water" (John 4:10; see verses 13–14).

That's right. We find Jesus here, wearied from His journey and sitting beside the well. But He wasn't there to drink; He was there to meet a woman who needed a drink. This Samaritan woman arrived to the well thirsty from the pressures of life and in search for a physical drink to satisfy her temporary thirst, but she didn't realize she was about to partake of Living Water that would quench her thirst on the inside. You may be reading this book, trying to satisfy a thirst with alcohol, only to find that it's temporary and you actually wake up thirstier than you were before. We can find ourselves so broken and thirsty that we don't even realize the drink we are turning to isn't good enough. We need something stronger, something that lasts. We need Living Water.

In just a few chapters, we find Jesus informing the people:

> On the last day of the feast, the great day, Jesus stood up and cried out, "If anyone thirsts, let him come to me and drink. Whoever believes in me, as the Scripture has said, 'Out of his heart will flow rivers of living water'."
>
> —John 7:37–38

The Living Water represents running water, water that is alive. It is a representation of the Holy Spirit. The moment you chose to drink from the well, to make Jesus the Lord of your life, you were "sealed with the promised Holy Spirit" (Ephesians 1:13). As a believer in Christ, you are sealed with the Holy Spirit. He is a gift to you.

You need the proper hydration to run the race God has called you to run. You cannot hydrate with a natural resource for a supernatural race. You need Living Water. You need the

Holy Spirit. He is your Guide, and He provides the directions you need for your race and so much more.

It is no accident that when Jesus was pierced on His right side while He hung on the cross, "at once there came out blood and water" (John 19:34). The very Spirit of God dwells in you. He is Living Water. He is your Source. When you recognize and depend on the Holy Spirit daily, you are drinking from the well of Living Water.

When you depend on the Word of God and the Holy Spirit, you are like a tree planted by streams of water (living water) that produces fruit in its time; your leaves do not wither, and you prosper in all you do (Psalm 1:2–3). Therefore, there is healing in the water, there is provision in the water, there is life in the water. You cannot run this race without it. You cannot fulfill your destiny without it. You cannot withstand the pressure or the training it will take without it. It is the very Holy Spirit who will keep you hydrated to endure the journey and give you longevity to endure the race. It is He who provides a way out and gives you strength to press on to the finish line. "Not by might, nor by power, but by my Spirit, says the LORD of hosts" (Zechariah 4:6). The oil we talk about, the anointing you hear about, the power of God—all of it comes from the precious Holy Spirit. What I have come to learn in my training is that He is all I have. He is my everything. People fail me, but He never does. The kind of peace He gives cannot be bought, nor given by man. If you are to make it through the trials, the valleys, the low places, then you need the proper hydration.

NUTRITION

When tackling a long-distance race, runners often take carbo-hydrate snacks to consume on the go to replenish energy stores and maximize the distance they are running. For example, when I set out on a twenty-mile run, I count how many carbohydrate snacks I will need based on the frequency I plan to consume them. That covers the fuel you need during the race, but what about while you are training for the race? What about on rest days—how do you fuel yourself? You can probably guess where I am going with this. The types of foods you eat while you train matter—even on the off days. You cannot gorge yourself on donuts and fried foods and expect to run the race well. You guessed it. The same diligence you take in fueling yourself with the right foods for the natural race is the same diligence you need for your spiritual food to run your spiritual race.

DAILY BREAD

In the Old Testament, we find the Israelites wandering in the desert and hungry. Yet God provided bread (manna) from heaven for them to eat. He provided daily bread—and not just any bread; this was holy bread. This was bread from heaven itself. I don't know about you, but I have never seen bread just fall from the sky with my own eyes. Fast-forward to the New Testament, when Jesus Himself became the Daily Bread. Just as we saw the woman at the well looking for water, we find the disciples looking for bread. We get a peek at this in John 6:

Jesus then said to them, "Truly, truly, I say to you, it was not Moses who gave you the bread from heaven, but my Father gives you the true bread from heaven. For the bread of God is he who comes down from heaven and gives life to the world." They said to him, "Sir, give us this bread always." Jesus said to them, "I am the bread of life; whoever comes to me shall not hunger, and whoever believes in me shall never thirst."

—John 6:32–35

You need daily bread. That means your nutrition is the Word of God—daily: "Man does not live by bread alone, but man lives by every word that comes from the mouth of the LORD" (Deuteronomy 8:3; see also Matthew 4:4). Just as we discussed in chapter 1, for you to feed your flame and keep your fire, you have to feed on the Word of God. Jesus is the "bread of life" (John 6:48).

For I received from the Lord Himself that [instruction] which I passed on to you, that the Lord Jesus on the night in which He was betrayed took bread; and when He had given thanks, He broke it and said, "This is (represents) My body, which is [offered as a sacrifice] for you. Do this in [affectionate] remembrance of Me." In the same way, after supper He took the cup, saying, "This cup is the new covenant [ratified and established] in My blood; do this, as often as you drink it, in [affectionate] remembrance of Me." For every time you eat this bread and drink this cup, you are [symbolically] proclaiming [the fact of] the Lord's death until He comes [again].

—1 Corinthians 11:23–26 AMP

Regardless of what you have been religiously taught, you have been given the gift of communion. You don't have to squat three times, run five laps, or confess your sins to other people in order to make yourself well enough to take communion. You have been cleared to partake of God's gift. You can freely receive it. The power is not in the actual elements—the cup of juice or the cracker. The elements are symbolic, but that is it. The power is in the actual partaking of the communion with thanksgiving and the posture of your heart. And who knows a man's heart but God. There is power in communion for overcoming doubt. There is power in communion for receiving physical healing in your body. There is power in communion as a remedy for every trial you face in your training. He is your Daily Bread, and feeding on (reading) His Word to get to know Him and remaining in His presence to discover the plans He has for you is all part of your training. Eat, for you have need of energy for the work ahead of you.

If you plan to get things done in life that will leave a legacy and make an impact, it will be a process. You will face obstacles. You will face trials, but through it all, if you are fueling yourself with the right ingredients, you will embrace longevity. I get it. Everyone has to start wherever they are, but I am not writing this for the faint of heart. If you truly want to get things done for God, run your race, and fulfill your destiny, it's going to take the Word and hard work. You need the Daily Bread so that when the enemy attacks with fear, doubt, or temptation, you can fight back with the Word. It is naïve to think that if you are about the Father's business, attacks won't come. Rather, they will come harder and faster—but if you are like that tree planted by streams of water and getting the proper nutrition to grow, you will not be moved, nor will you be shaken. You will not be easily toppled because your roots will be deep. When you get to mile twenty, you can speak the Word to yourself and be energized to run another four. Stay hydrated. Stay fed. Stay fueled. Let's keep running.

TRAINING QUESTIONS

1. What is your current process for fueling your fire? Is it working, or do you need to change it?

2. In what area of your life do you need to invite the Holy Spirit to quench the thirst?

3. Choose a Scripture that resonates with you and speaks to your situation, then memorize it.

4. Take a moment to pause, grab your communion elements, and partake of the Lord's Supper. Use this space to prayerfully record what you are believing God for as you partake of His Daily Bread.

MILE 11

HIDDEN

I have heard others say that their birthday is "just another day." Not me. It is a day to be celebrated. It is the day your Creator decided to schedule your grand debut into His creation. It is the day your life and your very breath would begin; after being hidden nine months in the womb, this is your grand debut.

On the morning of my birthday, the same day the Houston Astros would take home the 2021 ACLS title against the Boston Red Sox, I woke with a grateful heart and a deep sense of gratitude for the ability to run (physical health), the freedom to run (my country), and the dream of running (my purpose). I had such an overflow of joy and peace as I set out for an eight-mile run. My mind was on thoughts of God's goodness, and I was basking in His own proven faithfulness.

This particular morning, the dew was still on the ground. As I was running in the heavy mist of fog that lingered, something captured my attention through the thick haze. Although I could not quite make it out, I could see a faint image that looked like some sort of animal in the distance along my running path. As I drew closer, I noticed through the haze that there was more than one image—there was a pack of something that seemed to be huddled in the middle of the road. It was a like a showdown at high noon. I was coming for it, full steam ahead, and yet the pack wasn't moving. Whatever *it* was, it was standing still, staring straight at me. I began to slow my pace and my breathing to allow my eyes to focus and identify what exactly was hindering my running path this morning.

As I closed the gap with each step on the rugged terrain, the view became clearer through the misty air, and I saw the most beautiful sight. I was in awe. There was a herd of deer standing in the road, in the ditches, and off to the side of the meadow. I quietly came to a stop, slowing my breathing and pulling out my phone to take a picture of this amazing sight. The more I closed in on them, the keener their hearing became, and soon, I knew, they would run off into the woods, leaving me to run my intended course.

It was as if I could hear the Holy Spirit say, *Nothing is "hidden from [My] sight"* (Hebrews 4:13). Even though I couldn't see it, the fog had provided a covering to protect both them and me, and at the proper time we were both revealed. I couldn't help but be thankful for the opportunity to see such wonderful beauty—and on my birthday, too! It definitely was a birthday present from God, one He had wrapped neatly and covered in His mist of glory. With every stride, I saw an unwrapping taking place as I drew closer to the prize.

Our journey to your purpose and calling in life is a lot like this. The Master Planner wraps your plan, your victory, in His glory. With each stride you take as you run toward your destiny, your eyes come into focus, the vision becomes a little clearer, and each step is revealed, until all the mist is lifted and you finally realize that "no creature is hidden from his sight" (Hebrews 4:13).

HIDDEN BENEFITS

You are my hiding place;
you protect me from trouble.
You surround me with joyful shouts of deliverance.

—Psalm 32:7 CSB

My husband and I are polar opposites. He does not like to run. In fact, he jokes that if someone sees him running, they had better run, too, because something is definitely chasing him. Most people run to be hidden from attack, hidden from the enemy, seeking refuge and protection. Think of it as an American soldier in a foreign country who seeks shelter at the American embassy for solitude. Most people run to God when they know they are under attack, but what about when they have no idea they are under attack? Did you know that God still hides you even when you don't see the enemy lurking in the shadows? There is nothing hidden from the sight of your Fortress, which makes Him the ultimate hiding place, even when you are unaware you are being hunted.

HE IS MY HIDING PLACE.

The term *hiding place* used here in verse 7 in the original Hebrew language means "to preserve." While you may be interpreting "hiding" from your perspective as hiding from something or someone, your Master's perspective is that He is preserving you. What does it mean to preserve something? Not only does it mean "to protect and guard," but the word *preserve* also means "to reserve for a special purpose." Let that soak in, and read it again if you need to. Your Creator hides you for a reason, and He preserves you for a special intended purpose. When it is time for the unveiling, He will make sure you have the character to stay where He has intended you to be.

HE PROTECTS ME EVEN WHEN I CAN'T SEE THE ATTACK.

As a parent, I have set certain boundaries for my children. As they surf the internet and play games on their iPads, there are still boundaries within which they must remain. Those boundaries are not there to make their lives miserable or to make it seem like their mom just wants to be tough. The boundaries are there to protect them from the dangers that I know are out there, like online predators. Being the age of seven or younger, my children cannot comprehend what an online predator is; therefore, it is my job to make sure I have put boundaries in place to protect them. Your Creator does the same for you. You can't always see the dangers that lurk in the shadows or know what is ahead, but He does. He will provide you with that gentle nudge in the right direction to protect you and to preserve you for His special purpose. God's Word alone is a boundary map for how we are to live our lives and conduct our behavior. That direction provides us with supernatural protection and covering when we follow it, when we live it.

HE SURROUNDS ME WITH JOY.

The gift of joy cannot be purchased, but it comes from within. It is a virtue we must choose to operate in—much like patience. Joy follows gratitude. When was the last time you made a list of things, seasons, or people for whom you were grateful? There is joy to be found in the season of being hidden. I think of the famous Charlie Brown Christmas special in which Linus gives his speech and reads Luke 2:10: "Fear not: for, behold, I bring you good tidings of great joy, which shall be to all people." That great and hidden joy was a birth announcement—the birth announcement of Jesus. Like you and me, Jesus was hidden in the womb for nine months before He would make His grand debut. Instead of having fear of missing out on something or grumbling about whether you were noticed in the public view, choose to be joyful in the hiding place. Your Creator surrounds you with shouts of joy; He is rooting for you! He isn't hiding you away and being quiet about it. He is cheering you on when no one else is. When you don't hear the audible applause of man, you can rest knowing that your heavenly Father is in your cheering section. He is shouting with gusto for you to push through the process, endure the race, and strengthen your stance.

Let's dig a little deeper into the concept of "hiding." The hidden benefits are more than just being covered and protected. This is a place of refinement.

HIDDEN REFINEMENT

As your Creator hides you, He also refines you. Being hidden is a place of trial and testing; it gives you an opportunity to lean on and trust your Refiner. To *refine* something is "to make small changes to improve something; to make it more accurate." To *refine* also means "to remove unwanted elements or impurities." There are some things we should only want to be removed in private—am I right?

REFINER'S FIRE

When I hear the words *Refiner's fire*, there is a feeling in my bones to which words just cannot bring justice. Our Refiner uses fire, metaphorically speaking; He uses the trials and tests of life to get rid of the dross, the impurities, the unwanted excess, to cause us to shine brighter and become a sharper image of Himself. In biblical times, the word *refine* was associated with heating up silver and gold to a melting point in order to remove unwanted impurities and leave behind the desired luxurious elements of silver and gold. Take away the dross from the silver, and the smith has material for a vessel (Proverbs 2:4).

Our Refiner lets us know on multiple occasions in Scripture that He is refining us in the fire. There are many biblical heroes who come to mind who experienced the Refiner's fire, but one I want to bring to your attention is Joseph. His life was full of trials and testing, and he was hidden on more than one occasion. With each hidden season came new refinement. In Genesis 37, we find Joseph thrown into a pit, hidden in utter darkness, only to later be removed from the pit and then be sold into slavery. That's right—he was an example of biblical human trafficking. In Genesis 39, we meet up with Joseph again to find that he is now the overseer in charge of Potiphar's house; Potiphar was the captain of the guard in Egypt (kind of a big deal!). Life seems to be going well for Joseph despite his horrific past in which he was sold by his own brothers.

There was just one problem: Potiphar's wife had a lustful desire for Joseph. But Joseph was so loyal to his Refiner that he wouldn't have anything to do with her. Being the manipulative and deceitful woman she was, Potiphar's wife did the only thing she knew to do to save her reputation: She accused him of the unthinkable and had Joseph thrown into prison. Hidden again. After he spent years in prison, the opportunity eventually came for his gift to be used, which would unlock the door to release him from obscurity. A total of thirteen years expanded the gap between the time he was sold into slavery until the time he entered the service of Pharaoh and become the second in command over all Egypt. It would be another seven to eight years before he would be revealed to his brothers. Even in the unveiling and great reveal—after more than twenty years of refining—we see the posture of Joseph's heart coming out of the Refiner's fire.

> *And now do not be distressed or angry with yourselves because you sold me here, for God sent me before you to preserve life.*
>
> —Genesis 45:5, emphasis mine

145

How many people do you know who can be sold into slavery twice, then thrown into prison, only to be forgotten about for years, and still say after all that, "Don't be angry—God worked it all out for our good. He preserved me for such a time as this!" Joseph was able to surrender each season of hardship to the Refiner. In the surrender, we are able to allow God to remove the excess and shape our hearts and lives into who He has created them to be—to be more like Him.

My prayer for you as we close this chapter is that you would embrace your hiding place and reap the benefits of being hidden. Surrender your season of hiding to the Refiner and allow Him to renew a steadfast spirit in you, to cause you to burn brighter and become sharper than you were ever before. Remember that nothing is hidden from the sight of the Father, and He is in your cheering section, rooting for you! I am rooting for you, too. Keep running!

TRAINING QUESTIONS

1. How do you currently treat your birthday? Do you view it as just another day, if so why is that? How do you celebrate it?

2. What hidden benefit do you need to access in this season?

3. What impurities and excess waste do you need to allow the Refiner to burn away?

4. For what do you believe God is preserving you in this season?

MILE 12

ENDURANCE UNDER PRESSURE

You can tell a lot about someone's character by how they handle adversity. When you are hard-pressed with your back against the wall or under pressure to meet a deadline, how do you respond? In a season of pressure, you need endurance to produce the self-discipline that leads to the strengthening of your character. How I choose to respond when faced with challenges and trials says a lot about my ability to either have self-control or experience a lack thereof.

When I set out for an eighteen-mile run, it was about 45 degrees, with the sun shining brightly and moderate winds. At mile nine, the very tips of my toes began to ache, and my face felt frozen. I had thoughts of cutting the run short, and all sorts of justifications began running through my mind. They all sounded good ("it's too cold"; "you could get sick"; "that's enough for today"). On mile twelve, I noticed a lady in her yard who was trying to get my attention, so I slowed down, took out my earbud to hear, and leaned toward her. She yelled out, "I like your outfit!" Of course, I smiled, waved, and called out, "Thank you," but all the while, my Christian self was thinking,

I don't have time for this. I can barely breathe and run at the same time, let alone talk and try to run. Next, she asked, "Aren't you cold?" My response was, "Yes, ma'am, this is mile twelve, and I haven't warmed up yet."

On mile sixteen, I saw my own mother coming toward me on the road in her vehicle. She stopped to roll down her window and have a conversation. Mind you, it was brief, but still it was a distraction. I could have allowed any one of those distractions to cause me to quit before my goal was reached, especially the conversation with my mother. I only needed two more miles to finish, and if I recall our conversation, I am pretty sure she was on her way to eat pancakes (which is not only a distraction, but a temptation!).

I could have allowed the thoughts of being cold along with my achy body parts to stop me short and go eat warm, buttered pancakes with maple syrup. Yet, rather than exit too soon, I had to remind myself what I had set out to do in the first place and why I was running eighteen miles. I had a marathon scheduled in less than a month, and if I expected to complete it, then I needed to put my body into submission, as well as my mind and my thoughts, and discipline myself to reach the finish line.

Endurance is a word of which I believe most of us do not fully understand the meaning. Since you have hung with me this far, there is no reason you shouldn't finish. I took the time to write this chapter specifically on endurance under pressure to let you know there are times when each of us will experience an immense amount of pressure, whether internal or external, and that is when we need endurance the most. The pressure can make us feel stressed out and wanting to quit, or it can make us dig in our heels and work extremely hard. Some people work extremely well under pressure; in fact, they thrive under the pressure. Then there are those who collapse under the pressure. It simply is too much to bear. But what if I gave you a different way to view pressure? What if I told you that you could use the pressure to your advantage?

Please don't misunderstand me. This entire book, *Training Ground*, is about your need for endurance to run the race God has marked out for you. The entire premise of the book is that you must endure the process and discipline yourself to push through the challenges of different seasons of life to run your race and fulfill your destiny. In this chapter, I want to help you see how God uses the very thing that pressures you to create the power you need to forge ahead. Let's keep running.

The basic definition of *endurance* is "the ability to withstand hardship or adversity," *especially* "the ability to sustain a prolonged stressful effort or activity; a marathon runner's endurance."[12]

> *Therefore, since we are surrounded by so great a cloud of witnesses, let us also lay aside every weight, and sin which clings so closely, and let us run with* endurance *the race that is set before us.*
>
> —Hebrews 12:1, emphasis mine

> *Wherefore seeing we also are compassed about with so great a cloud of witnesses, let us lay aside every*

weight, and the sin which doth so easily beset us, and
let us run with patience *the race that is set before us.*

—Hebrews 12:1 KJV, emphasis mine

These two verses are the same, except the first is from the English Standard Version, which is easier to understand, and that is why I have included it for you. However, I want to also bring your attention to the King James Version. Here, the word *patience* is used in the place of *endurance*. I used to pray that God would give me more patience, and I bet if you are a parent reading this book, you've prayed for the same thing. I learned the answer to that prayer comes in the form of trials, which give you an opportunity to express and practice newfound patience. Needless to say, I now try to refrain from asking for patience; in a sense, it's like asking for more pressure! James tells us that we are already going to "meet trials of various kinds" (James 1:2), and I don't need any extra!

Endurance. Patience. Pushing through in the waiting season. Learning to wait is a lost art in a world that is fast-paced, a society in which everything we want to purchase, order, complete, or view can all be done in an instant on a device held in our very own hands. Let's think about this. You don't even have go to the grocery store now; they can be delivered to your house. You don't have to physically to go school on a campus anymore; you can take classes online and in some cases, micro-wave-style, if you get my drift. Can I just say that purchasing a certificate for fifty dollars in any area does not make you an "expert"; there is no "osmosis transfer" of knowledge. Yet, in this world we want everything *now*. We don't ever want to wait. We would rather leave and find a place where we can be served quicker or get our desire met faster. I find that as a parent, teaching patience to my children is difficult in this culture of Instant Pots. But here is the good part: Some things are just worth waiting for. That waiting period is called *process*. The waiting period doesn't mean you are doing nothing; it means you keep on running even when there is the pressure to quit. That waiting period requires patience. The word *patience* in the Greek language is *hupomone*, and it comes from the noun *hupomeno*, which means "to persevere," "to remain," "to bear up under."[13] The problem is that most of us quit when the pressure starts because pressure causes discomfort. When you focus on the pain and discomfort pressure brings, you take your eyes off the purpose the pressure was meant to serve. So, when adversity and opposition seem to be continuous, an exit route often looks appealing.

Early in my career as a registered nurse, I was extremely blessed with favor. At one time, I experienced a double promotion within a year. I experienced many blessings, but with them also came many persecutions, including hidden agendas and a "Judas" at the table. I was young both in age and in experience. I was not sure how to handle the situation without jeopardizing my character. I sought wise counsel and chose to stick it out, covering myself and my workplace in prayer. The Judas at the table made me want to quit every day! The Judas at the table was my boss, and I was the subordinate.

I could have easily decided to leave and find a different job. I could have easily quit. But I had just been promoted—not once, but twice. My salary had tripled in less than a year. I knew I wasn't supposed to leave. I was supposed to endure—not for the money, but for the power that would be forged through the process. I stayed. I submitted, and I gleaned a great deal from that Judas. I learned how *not* to lead. I learned how *not* to treat people. I learned how *not* to act at the table during a meeting. I learned how *not* to present myself. Most of all, I learned to forgive the Judas. I learned that a title will get you only so far, but that it takes character to sustain you. After enduring this Judas for almost four years, I was promoted yet again, and the wheels were reversed. Judas had become the subordinate. The pressure I experienced kept me humble;—it kept me persevering—and because of that, I was able to achieve yet another milestone that would take me closer to the fulfilling of my God-given purpose.

We are called to remain steadfast, secure, and sure of God's Word to see us through to the finish line. When you bear up under the pressure, even though what you really want to do is quit, you show courage, consistency, and character. When you bear up under the pressure, you make the devil angry. When you bear up under the pressure, you produce a power that can only be found from the making of oil in its purest form. Oil represents the power and presence of the Spirit of God, the anointing. To produce olive oil in its purest form, the olive must go through a process in which it is pressed. I can't help but think that as I am pressed through my own training ground in life, the very thing being produced in me is the power of God at work in my life. I believe He will use the very thing that is pressing you to produce power and breakthrough—if you will only endure the process and not quit.

One of my favorite stories in the Bible is found in 2 Kings 2:1–15. Here we find Elijah walking with his protégé, Elisha, on his final journey from Gilgal to Bethel. As I researched the distance between the two locations, several different ranges came in, anywhere from thirty-five to ninety-five miles. Let's just agree that either way, it was a long walk. Elijah knew his time here on earth was about to end, and so did all the spectators. Yet Elisha refused to entertain a word about it. Elisha refused to leave the side of his mentor and spiritual father, regardless of the naysayers on the sidelines and regardless of his own mentor's request for him to stay behind. Tucked away in this story, Elisha is provided with at least five opportunities to become discouraged, turn around, quit, and exit the route. The closer Elisha came to the end, the more frequent the opportunities to quit came. Nevertheless, Elisha remained steadfast, bearing up under the pressure to quit with a determination and resolve to see it through to the end. After seeing that his protégé would not give up, Elijah asked the question, "What can I do for you?" Elisha responded with the request for a double portion of Elijah's anointing, a double portion of God's power. "You have asked a hard thing. Nevertheless, if you see me taken from you, if you stick with me to the end and you stay focused, don't miss it, you will receive it," Elijah said. If you keep reading, you will find that Elisha did just that: he watched his mentor be taken from him in a whirlwind of fire and chariots. (I don't know about you, but that seems so epic—I want to go out like that!) Elisha saw Elijah through to the end, and the mantle was passed to him along with a double portion of the power and the anointing, and the Spirit of God then rested on Elisha.

Many people ask for this double portion of blessing, this double portion of power, yet few are willing to endure and pay the cost to receive it. Elijah knew the cost of the oil. That's why he let Elisha know he had asked a hard thing, meaning it was not going to be easy. The double portion anointing doesn't come cheap, and it isn't quickly cooked in a microwave oven. It will cost you. It comes through endurance of pressure, discipline, training, eating with Judas, walking by faith, and refusing to allow discouragement from others cause you to quit. It comes after being refined in the Refiner's fire.

Mile markers let us know how far we are and how far we have come in our journey. At each mile marker, we have the opportunity to make a choice. We can choose to keep running, or we can choose to stop. Elisha was faced with many mile markers of distractions that would give him the opportunity to choose to stop or to keep going. Just like he chose to keep going and follow Elisha to inherit the key to his destiny, I encourage you to keep going. I encourage you to grab your tools of self-discipline, faith, and resolve and press on through the pressure. Let's look at these tools a little closer:

SELF-DISCIPLINE

Don't you realize that in a race everyone runs, but only one person gets the prize? So run to win! All athletes are disciplined in their training. They do it to win a prize that will fade away, but we do it for an eternal prize. So, I run with purpose in every step. I am not just shadowboxing. I discipline my body like an athlete, training it to do what it should. Otherwise, I fear that after preaching to others I myself might be disqualified.

—1 Corinthians 9:24–27 NLT

Here the apostle Paul lets us know that in the natural race (a physical race), everyone is running for a material prize: The gold medal. The job title. The position. The promotion. Yet, in our spiritual race, the prize we are chasing is not material; it is eternal. When you are fulfilling your purpose here on earth, advancing the Kingdom of God, you will receive your eternal reward. You don't have to compete with the person in the other lane, for you have a crown all your own. However, just like runners train for a physical race, you, my friend, must train for your spiritual race—and that is called process. In this place of training, you must discipline yourself.

Self-discipline is defined as *the ability to control one's feelings and overcome one's weaknesses.*[14] Self-discipline is also defined as *the correction of oneself for the sake of improvement.*[15] Self-discipline is the ability to pursue what one knows is right despite temptations to do the opposite. That is so good. Let's unpack that. Have you ever felt emotionally hijacked? Have you ever felt like you were on an emotional roller coaster? Well, that's because you probably have been! Emotional intelligence expert Daniel Goleman coined the term *emotional hijacking* to describe when a part of our brain—called the amygdala, or the brain's emotional processing center—takes over our rational and normal reasoning, hence the emotional roller coaster.[16]

The good news is that there is a solution. We have been given God's Word. As Christ-followers, we are to be faith-led, not emotion-led. We recognize we have emotions, but we cannot allow those emotions to dictate our direction in life. Faith is the driver; emotions are riding in the backseat. Choose to respond by faith using God's Word. That, my friend, does not come naturally unless it has been practiced through self-discipline.

HIS WORD

God's will is His Word. Maybe you have heard this, too, or maybe you have thought this: *If the Lord's will is for me to be healed, then He will heal me, and if it's not, He won't.* Let me bring you some clarity. His will is His Word. His Word says that by His stripes you are healed. There is no room for a debate about whether you are healed or not; in the spiritual realm, you are already healed. It is your faith in His Word that activates the healing process. His Word says that if you ask anything in His name, according to His will, then you already know you have what you have asked (1 John 5:14–15). His will is for you to be healed, so speak that you are healed.

You may be thinking, *Well, I know someone who prayed for healing, but they weren't healed.* I can assure you, they received their healing in eternity. There are many things we may not see on this side of life, but that doesn't mean we should lose faith or hope. Some things we cannot explain. God is all-infinite and so much greater than our minds can comprehend. If we will discipline ourselves to hold steadfast to His Word, we can experience Him. Discipline yourself in the Word so that when temptation comes, you are able to resist it. Discipline yourself by training and conditioning your mind and body to endure and run the race you were called to run. If you are prepared, you will know how to respond when you meet Judas. If you are prepared, you will know how to respond when you are pressed.

WORSHIP

I love that God tells us He "inhabitest the praises" of His people (Psalm 22:3 KJV). This means that when I worship, God shows up to meet me. Worship can come in many forms; putting something first and idolizing it is a form of worship. Praying is a form of worship. Giving is a form of worship. However, in this context I want to talk about *your praise* being a form of worship in which you become disciplined. When you worship, you usher in the presence of God. When you worship, the enemy has to flee. When you worship, you can't help but be joyful and give thanks to God Almighty, the great I AM. He is whatever you need Him to be. Learn to worship at your house, in your car, outside, while you cook, while you clean. Get to the place of disciplined worship, where you find yourself singing without the music, making up your own song to just tell Him how good He is. Enter His gates with praise and thanks-giving—the "password [is] Thank you!" (Psalm100:4 MSG).

159

When you get to a place of worship and gratitude and start thanking Him for all the craziness from which He has kept you safe, the mountain you see in front of you begins to disappear, and you will find yourself strengthened with the ability to overcome with triumph until you see what you are believing for come to pass. Worship changes your atmosphere.

PRAYER

As we mentioned before, prayer is part of your training armor. Prayer is the single most effective weapon you have available in your arsenal. However, it only works when you use it. Prayer should be your first resort, not your last. Prayer is a form of communication and fellowship with the Lord that is personal and intimate. This is where you get to know the heart of the Father. He longs to meet with you. I think many times we make praying hard when it doesn't have to be. Prayers can be long, or they can be short. They can be loud, or they can be quiet. Prayer is all a matter of the heart. God considers the true intention behind the prayer, and whether or not you mean what you say and believe that you can have what you ask. Developing a disciplined prayer life is essential as you not only communicate with the Father, but you have the power to strike the mark and take out the enemy when the pressure is mounting against you. I encourage you to develop a habit of prayer. My prayer for you is that you would start praying and not stop. That you would pray without ceasing. That you would get to a place where your spirit man is constantly warring to endure and overcome. Prayer is essential.

FAITH

My brethren, count it all joy when you fall into various trials, knowing that the testing of your faith produces patience.

—James 1:2–3 NKJV

I think sometimes people—myself included—have read James 1:2 and seen it as a cliché, or "preachy" ("consider it pure joy, my brothers"—in my really preachy voice—"when you have trials of many kinds"). I mean, who really has joy and says, "Yes, I am so happy I am going through this marital conflict," or "I really see the joy in the face of this bankruptcy"? No one, right? Allow me to share with you what this means to me with new insight. "Faith cometh by hearing, and hearing by the word of God" (Romans 10:17 KJV). Faith produces patience. Faith produces endurance. Faith produces steadfastness. If I want faith, I have to speak God's Word, because when I speak God's Word, I hear it. When I hear God's Word, it fuels my faith, and when my faith is fueled, it causes a second wind to rise in me to keep going and endure. When I read God's Word and find out what He says about my situation and what He promises to do for me, I can't help but be joyful and renewed, able to endure the very thing I am pressing through.

I have included a few things God says He will do for me and for you. I purposely wrote them in the first person, so that when you read them, you can read it to yourself as such. Go ahead and read them out loud if you want to.

- He works all things out for my good (Romans 8:28).
- He perfects all things that concern me (Psalm 138:8).
- I have no need to worry, for in the day of trouble He will keep me safe in His dwelling. He will hide me in the shelter of His tabernacle and set me high upon a rock (Psalm 27:4).
- He justifies me (Romans 8:30).
- He vindicates me (Psalm 37:7).
- He protects me (Psalm 91:14).
- He shelters me (Psalm 91:1).
- He provides for me (Philippians 4:19).

He knows the end from the beginning, and He has already won. Therefore, I win, and I can praise Him before I see the victory because I already know that I have it! That, my brother or sister, is how I remain joyful and steadfast in the middle of a trial.

RESOLVE

Therefore do not throw away your confidence, which has a great reward. For you have need of endurance, so that when you have done the will of God you may receive what is promised.

—Hebrews 10:35–36

Resolve is defined as "reaching a firm decision."[17] When I think of having the type of determination that stems from the word *resolve*, I think about commitment: commitment to the process, commitment to the training plan, commitment no matter what. Commitment to run when it's cold and wet outside. Commitment to run when it's hot and humid. Commitment to finish my God-given race no matter the season. Resolve to stick it out even when it hurts, even when I don't see the result yet. To have this type of firm resolve takes confidence—confidence in who you are and to Whom you belong. To have this type of resolve takes backbone to stand your ground. The author of Hebrews urges us not to throw away our confidence, for we need it to endure the race.

Without resolve, you will take the nearest exit. Without resolve, you will be easily knocked over upon attack. Without resolve, you will leave a church because you were offended by someone else. Without resolve, you will quit easily because you don't like the environment. Without resolve, you will not reach your destiny.

Resolve will cause you to love someone despite their lack of love for you. Resolve will cause you to accept someone who rejects you. Resolve will cause you to forgive people when they don't even realize they need forgiveness. Resolve will cause you to run in the rain. Resolve will cause you to run no matter the condition of the environment. Resolve is needed to finish well. Resolve will cause you to discipline yourself in such a way that at the end you hear, "Well done, good and faithful servant."

I am reminded of the amazing story found in Daniel chapters 1–6. He was taken captive from his home as a teen and thrust into training to become like his captors. On the outside, he was handsome and chiseled with physique. On the inside, he resolved to remain firm in his belief to keep himself pure before God. He had faith that his God would rescue him. Daniel had developed a disciplined lifestyle of prayer. It was his custom to pray three times a day in a posture of worship. Approximately seventy years would pass from the time he was taken captive to the time his prayer life would be questioned. There was a group of people who were jealous of Daniel and his favor with the king. They sought to destroy him by issuing a decree that anyone found praying would be thrown into the lions' den. You see, even the enemy knew that Daniel's prayer life had become so disciplined he wouldn't be able to stop. This is the one trap he couldn't resist. When Daniel learned of the decree, he knew his only option was to pray. He took his posture and faced the Father, giving thanks, just as he had done many times before, for nearly eighty years. When his enemy captured him for violating the decree, he was thrust into the lions' den. But because Daniel had been so resolved in his faith, prayer, and posture of worship, God immediately shut the mouths of the lions.

I cannot begin to imagine the pressure Daniel must have felt when told of the initial decree. I cannot begin to imagine the pressure Daniel must have felt when trapped in the lions' den after being held in captivity for nearly eighty years. But I can imagine the power that was forged in him through his resolve. I can imagine that God would exceed his expectations and show up on the scene to rescue him. I want to be so effective and disciplined in my prayer life that when I'm eighty, the enemy knows about it.

Endurance under pressure is what causes God's power to be seen in you. Just like the olive is pressed for the purest form of oil, you are being pressed to produce the purest form of anointing that God has designed for you. Your pressure today will become your power source tomorrow. He will equip you for everything He has called you to do. He will provide you with everything you need to fulfill His plan and run the race He has marked out for you. My friend, discipline yourself, remain faithful, get in His presence, and stand with the resolve to see it through. I am praying for you!

TRAINING QUESTIONS

1. What pressures of life are you currently experiencing?

    a. Internal pressures?

    b. External pressures?

2. To what area of discipline can you commit for the next thirty days?

    a. Speaking God's Word over the situation you listed above?

    b. Worship?

    c. Praying over the situation you listed above?

3. What step of faith can you take to endure under the pressure you are currently experiencing?

4. Write a resolve statement on which you can later reflect to encourage you during the times of pressure.

MILE 13

BREAKTHROUGH PAIN

Some days are just hard. Some days are just tough. We don't deny or pretend that there isn't pain; we certainly recognize it. Yet God can use your pain to propel you forward for His glory.

> *And we know that for those who love God all things work together for good, for those who are called according to his purpose.*
>
> —Romans 8:28

He works all things out for our good—not just some things, not just the good things, but all things, even the messy stuff. I recommend that you post that where you will see it every day. Remind yourself that even in the situation you are going through right now, He will work things out for your good. I am not sure why we go through certain heartaches and pains, but I trust that God does. I am convinced that He uses even what the enemy meant for bad—He turns it around and uses it for His glory and for our good.

Much like pressure can be external or internal, so is pain. In relating pain to running, when you put your body through strict training and make it submit to a regimen every day that pushes it to its limits, you are bound to experience some sort of pain. Whether it is pain in your legs, muscles, and lower back, or whether your toes just hurt, there is pain. But anyone who runs and puts their body through that type of training doesn't just quit and say, "Well, I'm just not going to run anymore; it hurts too much." No, we may rest and take some time to recover, but we don't ever quit.

I don't want to minimize the pain of what you may be going through or have been through. I realize there is physical pain in our bodies that we feel during training that can make us want to sit it out. But what about when the pain is much deeper than a stubbed toe? What about the internal pain that you are not able to share with others. Your internal pain may stem from having to let go of something in order to make room for what God has for you. Your pain may go much deeper; perhaps your pain has been placed on public display for everyone to see. Your teenage daughter has become pregnant, your spouse has left you, you're facing financial stress, or your business is failing, and life just isn't going the way you planned it.

What about the pain you feel in the brokenness, hurt, and betrayal? Hurt and betrayal come in many different forms and at many different stages of life in many different seasons. I have been betrayed by friends and hurt by family members. I have seen God sever relationships, protect me, cover me, use my enemies as my footstools, and heal broken relationships through restoration and forgiveness. But there was usually pain first, and healing was a process that took time. In some instances, those processes are still being worked out, and in some areas, there are testimonies.

I struggle with what I want you to know in this chapter, mainly because there is a measure of vulnerability when it comes to exposing pain. It's raw. It's much easier to put a bandage over it so no one else sees it. It's much easier to keep going like it doesn't exist. The truth is, though, that pain left under all those bandages begins to ferment and grow infected, until it becomes bitterness and resentment.

I want you know that some training days are harder than others. Some training days will require you to remove a layer of bandage so you can face the pain and push through to your breakthrough. Some training days you will feel like giving up and throwing in the towel. Some training days are tough, but they are all worth it. I believe God uses our seasons of pain as fertilizer to bring forth fruit in our lives. I believe He works all things out for our good, so He uses our pain to bring out good fruit. He uses things like betrayal, death, and brokenness to bring out new life, new relationships, and new masterpieces. Pain may knock you down for a bit, but don't cover it up. Allow God to unwrap the bandages and face it head-on. Let Him heal you with grace and love so you can keep running.

In health care we have a term called *breakthrough pain*. It occurs in people who have chronic pain. Chronic pain is the pain that never really goes away, the pain with which we learn to live and function despite it. We often put layers of bandages over it. Now, breakthrough pain is not indicative of the root of the illness worsening, nor is it a sign there is a new condition present. Breakthrough pain takes place when there is a spike in the old pain, a sudden increase in pain in the same place. It usually lasts for a short period of time, but the awareness of it is very acute.[18] This is why people who experience chronic pain are prescribed breakthrough pain medication. Breakthrough pain medication is administered at certain intervals of time specifically to prevent breakthrough pain.

I once received a phone call from my mother to let me know that her father had passed away. She asked if I would please officiate the graveside service. She didn't ask for much. My mom and I have a close relationship, so I told her yes. For most people, the death of a grandparent would bring immense pain, but in my case, I did not have a relationship with him, which left no one to grieve at the time of his passing—or so I thought. I had only seen my grandfather twice that I could remember in my lifetime, once somewhere around the age of seven and then not again until the age of thirty-six. I never held it against him; he lived twelve hours away, and when I was old enough to drive and had a family of my own, I could have easily made travel arrangements to go see him to try to build a relationship.

I, along with my brother and mother, traveled to West Texas to attend a funeral for a man who seemed like a stranger. I was preparing myself to officiate a funeral for my grandfather, a man I hardly knew. As I reflected in the travel time, pondering what to say at the service, I wasn't sure I had actually lost anything. Yet I still felt a sense of emptiness. When I saw my mom at the graveside, I knew what it was. Abandonment. She was experiencing breakthrough pain, a sudden increase in pain from the chronic problem of abandonment. Because just like I hadn't known my grandfather, she hadn't seen her father, and now the long-distance relationship she'd had by phone for the last forty years was being unwrapped layer by layer. And as a woman who is now also a mom, I couldn't help but wonder what she must be feeling, the emotional roller coaster she must have been on, the "what ifs" that rolled through her mind, the pain of her parents' divorce and events that could have and should have been avoided that would later serve to produce her own "oil." I was reminded that God is a Father to the fatherless. I was also reminded that before there is breakthrough, there is often pain.

That event in West Texas caused me to let go of the pain that had become a feeling of abandonment. That event gave my mother a breakthough in the midst of her breakthrough pain. Even when your natural father falls short, your heavenly Father "will never leave you nor forsake you" (Hebrews 13:5). He fills any void, He covers any emptiness, and He is fully present. He is the great "I AM" (Exodus 3:14). Whatever you need Him to be in your moment of pain, He is. He is your breakthrough. Rest assured that your pain is not the end; there is more. Break through your pain to give birth to your purpose.

In 2 Samuel 5, we get a glimpse of David dealing with the pain of his own long-standing enemy, the Philistines. This was the same group of people whom he had been battling since he had slayed Goliath as a youth. Now he was a man in search of his breakthrough to overcome his long-standing enemy.

171

Rather than cover it up with more bandages, he was asking the Lord for direction concerning his next battle: "Will You be with me if I face them? Will You deliver me?"

Of course! Our Lord of Hosts assured David of his victory and delivered him just as He said He would. For his victory dance, David recorded the place as *Baal- Perazim*, and he said, "The LORD has broken through my enemies before me like a breaking flood" (2 Samuel 5:20). In Hebrew *Baal-Perazim* means "the Lord has broken out."[19] Now, I don't know about you, but that makes me just sit in awe. Wow, my God is the Lord of the Breakthrough! You are in a place where the Lord has broken out.

When a woman goes into labor, there is pain. There is water that must break, allowing the stages of labor to advance and progress. It is not until her water is broken and she is at a certain stage in her pain (labor) that she is directed to push. There is pain she must push through and water that must break to receive the gift of life. Like a woman who goes into labor, so must we labor for our destiny, but rest assured, there is breakthrough, and on the other side is the gift of life.

I don't know what your chronic pain is or if it's a new pain, but I am here to declare to you that your water has broken! Push! Push through your pain to experience your breakthrough. The God you serve is the Lord of the Breakthrough! There is new life on the other side waiting for you; you need only to push through and seize it.

> But he said to me, "My grace is sufficient for you, for my power is made perfect in weakness." Therefore I

will boast all the more gladly of my weaknesses, so that the power of Christ may rest upon me. For the sake of Christ, then, I am content with weaknesses, insults, hardships, persecutions, and calamities. For when I am weak, then I am strong.

—2 Corinthians 12:9–10

The apostle Paul shares these words with us at a time when he is begging God to remove the very thing that is causing him pain. Yet instead of removing the pain, God causes Paul to recognize His presence in the pain and draw on the Spirit of God to strengthen him in the area of his pain. What if, instead of asking God to remove the pain, you recognize the Spirit of God and His strength at work in you to overcome the pain, to push through? That is where the testimony of strength and victory come in. It's not that the pain was just removed, but it's all about the power that was forged out of the pain through our recognition of the hand of God. When we understand God's grace and we are able to receive it freely and rest in it, we can push through the pain because we know that God's power and strength is made perfect in us. In other words, it's in the vulnerable places that God shows us His best work. When you allow yourself to rest in God's grace, it actually removes the heaviness, and it releases the bandages, layer by layer. It is here that you feel the release. It's here that the freedom sets in. It's here that you find the strength to push through for your breakthrough.

Now the Lord is the Spirit, and where the Spirit of the Lord is, there is freedom.

—2 Corinthians 3:17

TRAINING QUESTIONS

1. What pain are you currently facing?

    a. Internal:

    b. External:

2. Have you layered so many bandages over the pain, that now it has turned into something deeper? Explain.

    a. Offense:

    b. Resentment:

    c. Bitterness:

    d. Anger:

3. For what breakthrough are you currently believing?

4. I challenge you to receive God's grace today. Allow Him to remove the layers of bandages and heal your hurt. Whom do you need to forgive today?

ADAPTABILITY

There is a trail race in Texas that occurs in August—the hottest part of the year, in my opinion. If you are from Texas, you know that we have summer, and then we have August. Let me preface this with the fact that there are plenty of aid stations and volunteers to make sure the race is done safely. Everyone is strictly monitored to ensure proper hydration. Most races start early in the morning—between 5:00 and 7:00 a.m. This particular race purposely starts at twelve noon and is held in a hot and dry place. The intent of the race is to test the runners' ability to adapt and endure under the pressure of the heat. Thus far, we have covered how you can adapt your training to different environments. We have discussed different weather conditions and preparation with the proper fuel, hydration, and equipment. Just like running when the terrain is different, we also must take time to adjust to the altitude the higher we climb the mountain of our destiny. One process in your training ground is your *adaptability*.

In life, as you run your God-given race, you will have to learn to adapt in different situations, different seasons, and different environments. There are three keys to adaptability I want you to have in your training, so that when the pressure is on, when the turn is sharp, and the altitude changes, you can adapt. Adapting in the situation does not mean that you should lower your standard of living and compromise who you are to be like others. Adapting means that you relate to the situation, to the people, and that you are flexible in your plan while still being true to who you are.

ABIDE

I am the true vine, and my Father is the vinedresser. Every branch in me that does not bear fruit he takes away, and every branch that does bear fruit he prunes, that it may bear more fruit. Already you are clean because of the word that I have spoken to you. Abide in me, and I in you. As the branch cannot bear fruit by itself, unless it abides in the vine, neither can you, unless you abide in me. I am the vine; you are the branches. Whoever abides in me and I in him, he it is that bears much fruit, for apart from me you can do nothing. If anyone does not abide in me he is thrown away like a branch and withers; and the branches are gathered, thrown into the fire, and burned. If you abide in me, and my words abide in you, ask whatever you wish, and it will be done for you. By this my Father is glorified, that you bear much fruit and so prove to be my disciples.

—John 15:1–8

There is so much in this passage of Scripture that simply a section in a chapter does not do the text justice. Yet my hope is that you see the benefits of abiding in the Master. Know that the entire premise of this beautiful concept of grace between the branches, the Vine, and the Vine Dresser is process—the process of remaining, pruning, and producing. To abide is to remain, to follow a certain plan or course of action despite the trials and temptations. I like to think of *abide* as sticking to the race (spiritual and physical) and running no matter what.

Jesus reminds us in His very own words that when we abide in Him, He abides in us, and we can bear much fruit (John 15:4). In other words, if we remain in Jesus and in His Word, and if we have faith in His Word, He will make sure that we see His promises fulfilled in our lives. He will prove Himself faithful. When we stick to God's plan for our lives, heeding His direction, He gives us what we ask for. When I abide in Him, I become more like Him, formed in His image. When I abide in Him, I realize there isn't anything I have gone through that He hasn't already gone through Himself. And not only did He go through it before me, but He goes through it with me now. He can relate to me, and I to Him.

When I can relate to Him, and He to me, I can relate to others and adapt in different situations. Adapting to others in their situations means to relate to them through the Father. Because I abide in Jesus, and He has been where I have been, He has been where they have been. He has been where *you* have been. When we can relate to Jesus because we have remained in Him, we can relate to others. Adapting in different environments and relating to others from different backgrounds other than our own gives us the ability to connect with people. And when you can connect with people, you have the ability to influence people. When you influence people, you have the ability to transform the world around you for God's glory.

As we abide in Him, we experience the blessing, but we also experience the pruning. Although it may not feel like it at the time, the pruning is a blessing, too. In the second verse, the True Vine lets us know that "every branch in me that does not bear fruit he takes away, and every branch that does bear fruit he prunes, that it may bear more fruit" (John 15:2). Pruning is part of the growth process; there are branches in your life that have to be cut back even if they are producing fruit.

Several years ago, my grandmother gave me a small rosebush in a planter that she had grafted from her mother's original rosebush. I planted the tender plant near our back porch so that it would get the best portion of the morning sun. The rosebush eventually grew to over five feet tall, withstanding Hurricane Harvey and the notorious Texas freeze. I noticed that the bush was tall, but thin. There were budding stems of pink roses, but the bush wasn't full. When I consulted with a friend who owns a nursery, I explained to her that I had been afraid to trim the bush back for fear of killing the bush—which had been alive for now three generations—to which she answered that pruning was the only way it would grow into all it was meant to be. My dear friend recommended I cut it back—half of its current size. So I did. Three months after the pruning process, the rosebush multiplied its stems and blooms, and it has never been so full since the day I brought it home in the small pot.

Friend, our Master Vine Dresser prunes us not just for our benefit, but for the benefit of the next generation and those connected to us. Our Master Vine Dresser knows just how much to cut back and where—not just so we can produce more fruit, but so that we can grow into all that we were meant to be. Where is the Master Vine Dresser pruning you? Is it in the area of your finances? Is it in a relationship or in the workplace? Allow Him to cut you back in this season, so that you can flourish in the next.

ABASE

The apostle Paul was saying that he not only knows what it is like to suffer lack and to have plenty, but he also knows how to be content in each situation.

> *I know how to be abased, and I know how to abound. Everywhere and in all things I have learned both to be full and to be hungry, both to abound and to suffer need. I can do all things through Christ who strengthens me.*
>
> —Philippians 4:12–13 NKJV

To *abase* means "to be humbled, reduced, brought low, or lack necessities."[20] Abasement can be used as a pruning process. I like to think of it as being content without all the extras. The truth is, for me, we have been extremely blessed. When my husband and I got married, we both had good jobs and a nice

181

starter home, but making ends meet was still tough. Reality set in when bills started rolling in, and all of a sudden we went from being independent to having a joint checking account and making joint decisions. I went from shopping for an extra pair of shoes to rolling change to buy groceries. I look back at how far we have come, though, and to be honest, I have more of an amnesia factor to the entire situation, because I don't think it was that bad. I honestly felt content. I knew God would take care of us no matter what, because we operate on His economy. So, if you find you are in a place with lack or struggle, and you feel yourself suffering, let this serve as a reminder: if you abide in Him, and He in you, you will bear fruit, and even after you have been cut back, you will bear more fruit than before.

> *For everything there is a season, and a time for every matter under heaven.*
>
> —Ecclesiastes 3:1

Just like there are seasons throughout the year—spring, summer, fall, and winter—there are different spiritual seasons. When I think of an abasing season, I think of a dry season, a hot season, like summer.

Running in the summertime can be dangerous. If you are not used to the South Texas heat, let me just tell you, it's *HOT!* What are some of the dangers? Overheating, sunburn, and dehydration, to name a few. When we get to this dry place spiritually, we run the risk of becoming complacent and sedentary, because it would be much easier to forgo training and stay where it's comfortable. It would be much more enticing to stay indoors, on the couch, binge-watching our favorite television shows. Yet what should we do in the dry season? Keep running. There is training in the dry season, the season of abasing. In fact, it is the most fertile place to experience our blessing, and it's the best training ground. The dry place is where we can hear God. The dry place is where our fire burns and spreads wildly. The dry place is where God shows off His miracles. Let me show you.

A simple definition of a dry season is little to no rainfall, or a lack of water. It is here, in the dry season, that you end up with no trees or production of fruit. During Bible times, there was no grocery store with curbside pickup; people lived off the agriculture—the sowing season and the harvest season—and livestock to feed their families. Imagine hardened, dry ground with cracks your foot could slip through. The dry air removing the final remnants of moisture from your skin. A famine. No rain. No farming. No harvest. No animals—because they are pushed to leave to find where any supply of water might be. Now think of life today. Our drought would look a little different, but not by much. To us, the grocery stores would have no supplies, and perhaps there would be a conservation of free-flowing water from the kitchen sink. But what about life? What about seasons of emptiness when the well of life has run dry, you experience lack, and you find yourself in a barren season, a season of drought?

The dry season is a preparation season. This is the time you use to lean into God, to hear Him more clearly, to expect Him to sprout a blessing in the drought. The unexpected happens on dry ground. God created man from dry ground and breathed life into him (Genesis 2:7). God spoke to Moses through a burning bush in the dry place (Exodus 3). Moses led the Israelites out of slavery, and they crossed the Red Sea on dry ground (Exodus 14). Jesus grew up like a *tender shoot,* "like a root out of dry ground" (Isaiah 53:2). Jesus Himself was birthed in a dry place. Elijah and Elisha crossed the Jordan River on dry ground (2 Kings 2). Your Redeemer can grow the *unexpected* out of dry ground or in a dry place.

There is a story tucked away in Exodus 17:1–7. Here we find Moses and the Israelites journeying through the wilderness. After traveling for quite some time, they finally made it to camp, yet they had nothing to drink. Can you imagine the exhaustion and the weariness? Can you imagine finally coming to a resting place after running your first marathon, only to have no water to drink? Rather than believe God for the provision of water, even after all the miracles the nation had witnessed, they chose to grumble. The posture the Israelites took was one of complaint rather than praise. Yet God still proved Himself. God commanded Moses to strike the rock with the same staff that had been used to demonstrate God's power and provision as he led the nation out of slavery. Check out his exact words:

Behold, I will stand before you there on the rock *in Horeb; and you shall strike the rock, and water will*

come out of it, that the people may drink. And Moses
did so in the sight of the elders of Israel.

—Exodus 17:6 NKJV, emphasis mine

Did you catch that? The part where God says, "I will stand before you there on the rock"? Hold on to that for a moment. Let's fast-forward to where we find the apostle Paul reminding the Church what God did for the Israelites. He reminded the Church that the Israelites were in the wilderness, and all ate the same spiritual food, "and all drank the same spiritual drink. For they drank from the spiritual Rock that followed them, and the Rock was Christ" (1 Corinthians 10:4).

I can't help but wonder, if the Israelites hadn't been so distracted with how they felt and what they didn't have, would they have seen God standing at the rock? If the Israelites had just had a different posture, one that desired to fulfill their purpose, one that desired to trust the Promise Keeper, one that desired to follow the Way Maker with gratitude and praise rather than grumbling and complaint in the abasing season, would they have realized they had access to the Rock of Living Water to satisfy their thirst? The entire nation missed it, so much so that an entire generation had to die off before they could enter the Promised Land. I don't know about you, but I don't want to miss it. I don't want to miss what God is trying to do now. I don't want to miss what God wants to reveal in this season for my generation or the next.

Even in the dry season, God is trying to get your attention. He is your Source. He is your Rock. He is your Well of

Living Water. He is your Sprout in the Drought. What have you been distracted with that has caused you to miss seeing God right in front of you, standing at the very rock from which He will supply your provision? What have you been so focused on not having that you have forgotten to give thanks for what you *do* have? What have you been barren of in this season? Start seeing your place of barrenness as your place of harvest. Start seeing your dry place as a place of provision. Start seeing your wilderness as a place of miracles and burning bushes. Start seeing your rock as the Rock of Ages, the firm foundation on which you stand, the endless supply of Living Water. I hear God saying, "There is a Sprout in the Drought!" Start seeing your season of abasement as a season of preparation for abundance.

ABOUND

To *abound* means "to exist in large numbers or to have plenty."[21] This is the season of abundance! This is the season of more than enough. Remember my fourth-generation rosebush? It is abounding with rose blossoms after its pruning season. Adaptability in the abundance season is just as important as it is in the abasement season. Abiding in Him is just as important in the abounding season as it is in the dry place, lest pride fill your own eyes for your achievements.

If we are not careful, we will forget about God in the seasons of abundance, when everything is going well. When we forget, we lose our adaptability, and things quickly begin to spiral out of order. A side effect of misplacing God on the order spectrum will cause us to become emotionally led, and we will soon view the very thing we asked for as a curse rather than a blessing.

Consider, for example, that you have just been blessed with the new home for which you spent time praying. Then, after a year or so, upkeep is required. Plumbing fixtures quit working. There is a leak in the roof, and all of a sudden, you can't stand the house, because you are cursing the very upkeep it's requiring. As you abound in abundance in the overflow of blessing, remain in Him. Abide in Him so that in every situation, you may adapt.

At the ripe old age of twenty-eight, I became an assistant vice president, and then a chief nursing officer at the age of thirty-one. I remember walking into my executive office for the first time and feeling such gratitude and reverence for what God had done. He had quadrupled my salary in a matter of three years—there was an abundance. There were also times when I had misplaced God on the order spectrum during the season of abundance, and I quickly began to see my newfound authority and position as a curse rather than a blessing. I was trying to do it all in my own strength, and eventually I found myself on the brink of burnout. That's when the gentle whisper of the Holy Spirit brought forth the words that seem all too familiar: *You can do all things through Christ who strengthens you* (Philippians 4:13). As I looked up the verse for myself, I noticed the verse before it. Let's look at it again, in case you missed it the first time:

I know how to be brought low, and I know how to abound. In any and every circumstance, I have learned the secret of facing plenty and hunger, abundance and need. I can do all things through him who strengthens me.

—Philippians 4:12–13

The apostle Paul was reminding us that we have to learn how to be blessed and still abide in Him so that we operate in His strength and not our own, even in the seasons of abundance. As you abound in the season of abundance, remember where you have come from in the abasing seasons that you come to appreciate and abide in the *Blesser* and not just the blessing.

As God calls you to expand your reach and increase your influence for His Kingdom, adaptability will be required of you. Learning to adapt in different seasons of life is what gives you the key of relatability and connection to others. Maybe you are like me, and you build walls around hurt and situations that you care about as a protection mechanism, until one day you realize you have become a prisoner in the very walls you built for yourself. I can relate. I also know that if you can relate to that, you won't be vulnerable with just anyone. You will only be vulnerable with those who relate to you, who have been where you have been—and even then you will still be guarded. You see, what I have learned—and I am still learning—is that we cannot present ourselves so holy and righteous, as if we have never been through anything that we come across as untouchable and impenetrable. Being willing to share your pain, where you have been, and how far you have come is what others can relate to. But most of all, being a witness to what God has done for you, giving God the glory for how He brought you out of the dry season and into the season of abundance—that is what increases your adaptability. When you are able to give God the glory in every situation and in every season abide in Him, be it abasing or abounding, you increase your adaptability.

TRAINING QUESTIONS

1. Where is God asking you to adapt in this season?

2. What key element of adaptability resonates with you the most?

    a. Abide:

    b. Abase:

    c. Abound:

3. Where is God currently pruning you?

4. Do you find you have trouble relating to others? If so, what can you do differently?

MILE 15

STRETCH

One of the activities in which I love to participate with my children is CrossFit. Getting them to work out is easy; they actually love it. The hardest part is getting them to stretch. In the moment, we really don't see the benefits of stretching, and we may wonder if it really works. It isn't until after we have stretched consistently that we begin to notice our increase in flexibility and mobility. My eight-year old son, full of energy and zeal, completed his workout of the day with exuberance. When he was finished, he reached down to touch his toes, only to find the tightness behind his knees had limited his mobility, rendering him uncomfortable. Stretching is uncomfortable.

I return to the woman-in-labor analogy we discussed in the chapter concerning breaking through your pain. When a woman becomes impregnated with life, the seed begins to form slowly, stretching her body in ways it has never been stretched before. For nine months, as she carries the weight of an extra human life, her insides begin to stretch. That which you can't see first begins to stretch. Her muscles stretch. Her hip bones and pelvis stretch and position themselves in ways that can handle the upcoming breakthrough. Her skin begins to stretch, maximizing its potential to bring forth new life. As the time draws near, she becomes increasingly uncomfortable. As her body stretches during the birthing process to deliver new life, soon her skin is marred by the stretching, and it is evident that she has been stretched to fulfill a purpose.

Becoming uncomfortable causes growth on the inside that manifests itself like a scar on the outside. We often don't see the growth in ourselves on the inside; it may take someone on the outside looking in to point it out. When I see others growing in their purpose, making strides for the Kingdom, I can often see where they have been stretched. I've seen the older gentleman, quiet in nature, reserved in stature, yet stretched to pray openly for others. I have seen women stand to give their testimony and begin to weep because of the stretch it takes to be vulnerable and show their battle scars. Be it a natural scar from a physical stretching or a spiritual scar from internal growth, stretching leaves a mark. It's a good mark, though. It's a mark that says, *I have been stretched for my God-given purpose. I was stretched to get here.* Like a rubber band is stretched to serve its purpose, so are you.

For a short season, I served as the youth pastor at our local church, which by far has been one of my greatest stretches. While the season was shorter than I anticipated, it stretched me in ways I never would have stretched myself logically, both literally and spiritually. The entire season was uncomfortable for me. I was stretched in sermon preparation. I was stretched to hear criticisms in love, only meant to make me better. I was stretched in the battle of my mind as I questioned my calling. What I learned was that even though I didn't stay in that season long and it didn't turn out like I expected it to, God still used it to stretch me and grow me in ways I never thought possible. He made room for the *Training Ground*. That season of stretching left me with a mark that says, *God qualifies the called*. As I am running my God-given race, I have come to know there are different seasons that require stretching in different places.

THE PRE-STRETCH

Most runners know that stretching before and after a run is one of the most valuable uses of your time, and it always should be done. Stretching is often uncomfortable or boring, and we may wonder, *Does it really help?* A proper warmup and stretch prior to your run will help to prevent muscle injuries. As your body sits idle, your muscles shorten. When you take off running, your brain sends messages to your muscles, requesting them to lengthen the strides. Without the proper preparation and stretching before you run, there is a greater risk for injury.[22] Stretching is essential.

The pre-stretch is the stretch before the run. This is the stretch that prepares you for the long haul of endurance. The pre-stretch will enable you to run farther with ease. The pre-stretch will decrease the likelihood of an injury that could cause you to forfeit the race or delay your destiny.

There are differences in opinions on stretching before and after a physical race, just like there are differences in opinions on the types of stretches, including a static stretch versus a dynamic stretch. An example of a static stretch is the basic bend-down-and-touch-your-toes-for-thirty-seconds type of

193

stretch, whereas dynamic stretches are designed to provide movement in the stretch, properly warming up the muscle groups you will be using during the run. An example of a dynamic stretch is to extend your arms out to the side, then rotate forward and backward in small, circular motions, gradually making larger circles. The right types of stretches for your exercise modality are key to having a successful workout and race.[23]

The right type of pre-stretch for your God-given race is just as important. Sometimes we know what we are stretching for, and other times we can't see what we are stretching for—but God knows exactly where and when to stretch us. The pre-stretch is usually exciting. The pre-stretch prepares you for the new season on which you are about to embark, whether that's a new business, a new marriage, or a new ministry. You want to be around people who will stretch you to fulfill your purpose.

My pastor is gifted in stretching people. He will stretch you out of your comfort zone to prepare you for what God has in store for you. He recognized the pastoral gift inside me, but he didn't just give me an opportunity to speak on the Sunday when he recognized the gift. He stretched me first. I started serving in the nursery, where I taught toddlers on their level. From there I graduated to speaking to women on Wednesday nights as a fill-in for our First Lady. It wasn't until my faithfulness proved itself that I was given the opportunity to stretch yet again and speak on a Sunday morning. All three stepping-stones were a type of stretching for me. The nursery would stretch my patience and ability to phrase the text in a way a child could understand. The women's ministry would stretch me in preparing a message and then delivering it to a crowd of my peers. The Sunday morning service would stretch me in ways that only a pastor would understand—and the youth ministry? Well, it, too, would stretch me in ways that only a youth pastor would understand. My point is, stretching is always required before you run.

THE MIDDLE STRETCH

After a while, when the "new" fizzles out and you find yourself wandering in the mundane, in the pain, and in the process, you can bet you are "in the middle." This is where you need endurance the most.

As you are running this race of life and fulfilling your God-given purpose, your faith is stretched in the process. You are stretched in the middle to get out of your comfort zone and grow in areas in which you wouldn't necessarily choose to grow. Faith is required to trust for God's provision when you don't see it. Stretching in the middle activates God's power. While it may feel exhausting in the middle, and you aren't sure whether to turn back or keep going, let me assure you there is power in the middle stretch.

In the book of Exodus, we see Moses in the middle of his journey to lead the Israelites out of slavery. Their faith is stretched in the wilderness as the children of Israel had to depend on Yahweh to provide. With every provision God supplied, there was an instruction to stretch. Moses was instructed to stretch out his hand, only for us to visualize the manifest miracles that would lead to freedom and provision.

Another example is found in Mark 3:1–6, where a man with a withered hand, after stretching out that hand, received restoration and healing. I can't help but wonder what went through the minds of these two men who stretched out their hands at the command of their Master. Moses must have wondered, *Will it work?* The man with the withered hand might have had insecurities about what onlookers would say about him as he stretched out his deformity for all to see. What would people think? What would people say? Stretching requires change, and change can bring out opinions and ridicule from the crowd. But if you have the tenacity to activate your faith and the obedience to stretch anyway, you will see the power in the stretch.

Now that you have warmed up and starting running, there is still stretching that occurs during the run. This type of stretching occurs by default. For example, when you run, your muscles elongate (stretch), and eventually it becomes a little easier to run. You aren't necessarily trying to stretch; your body is being stretched in the process as you run. Whether you are stretching physical muscle groups while preparing to run or stretching your faith in the process of receiving God's provision, stretching is required. One thing I know for certain is that stretching releases power. If you find yourself in the middle, stretch. The middle is where endurance kicks in and brings a second wind. Your *Training Ground* is in the middle. If you will continue to push through and access the miracles in the middle, you will reach the celebratory end with the excitement all over again at completion. Don't turn back or give up in the middle, but keep running, and keep stretching. It is in the stretch that we grow and enlarge our tent pegs to expand our reach.

THE POST-STRETCH

The post-stretch is a celebratory stretch. Here you take the time to enjoy the victory and the contentment of completion. As you are running your God-given race and fulling your destiny, there will be different seasons, chapters, and milestones of the journey. With each one, there is stretching, and the stretching at the end of a season allows you to celebrate and make room for growth. In the biblical era, wine was made by pouring new wine into new wineskins. The wineskin was made up of the hide of an animal. Then, once the wine was poured into the wineskin and stored, fermentation would take place. As the wine fermented, the wineskin stretched. The stretch occurred after the wine was poured. Much like a balloon stretches as it is filled with air, the wineskins also were stretched. As the process took place, the stretching occurred. And once the process was finished, the wineskin lost its elasticity.[24] Now, the difference between you and the actual wineskin is that the old wineskin was disposed of once it lost its elasticity, because they could no longer put new wine in the old wineskin or the skin would burst. You, however, must put away old habits and stretch again to enter the next season.

Just like after a long-distance run, the cooldown of your muscles and post-stretching are required. The post-stretch prevents muscle stiffness and reduces soreness. The post-stretch speeds up the healing process and makes the transition to recovery smoother. Another reason for the post-stretch is to make room for growth. After I ran my first full marathon—26.2 miles—I walked for a bit, but then I stretched for a long while to allow myself time to recover before I began the trek back to the car. That stretch allowed me to recover faster for days to come. As you fulfill your purpose to run your race in life, don't skip the stretching. The stretching makes room for grace, gratitude, and growth: Grace to complete what you have started. Gratitude for the freedom to run. And growth to maximize your potential, both spiritually and physically.

TRAINING QUESTIONS

1. Who stretches you to reach your God-given purpose?

2. When was the last time you were stretched out of your comfort zone, and what did you learn?

3. In what season of stretching do you find yourself right now?
   a. Pre-Stretch
   b. Middle Stretch
   c. Post-Stretch

4. What old habits do you need to do away with in order to make room for growth in the next season?

THE THREE CS

Do you not know that in a race all the runners run,
but only one receives the prize? So run that you may
obtain it.

—1 Corinthians 9:24

After all the races I have run, I always get asked two questions: "What was your time?" And, "what place did you come in?" I can tell you I dislike both of those questions. I have never liked those questions, because I never ran for competition. Upon embarking on my running journey, I never thought I would win a race—I just wanted to beat my own time. I was in competition with myself.

When I began to educate myself on the other runners in the same race that I was running, I learned there are "ultra-runners" who are running for the gold medal. These elite runners are incredibly fast and seasoned in endurance to obtain the prize at the end, yet still, for some of them, the only competition is themselves.

As for me, I knew I would never be able to keep a seven-minute-per-mile pace for 26.2 miles in order to keep up with these elite runners. Therefore, my only real competition is me. Did I beat my time from the last time? How can I be a better version of me? Those are the questions I would like to answer.

As you are training for your God-given race, you will be tempted with two of the three Cs: *competing* and *comparison*. After reading this chapter, I hope you walk away with tools to combat the temptation and learn the third and ultimate C: *co-labor*.

COMPETING

I'm not a competitor by nature—okay, maybe just a little bit. But I bet I know a few natural competitors, and so do you. You might be a natural competitor yourself! Not all competition is bad. I do believe there is healthy competition. Healthy competition is that which makes each competing party better. It creates a drive in you to become better, to grow, and to achieve. Healthy competition isn't one-sided; both parties in the competition benefit.

Unhealthy competition, on the other hand, is competition that says, "I want to be bigger and better than you at any cost." This type of competition drives people to cut corners, become deceitful, and tear others down, and it actually creates division. Competition borne out of arrogance and spite is driven by pride. This type of competition doesn't just show up on the track or the sporting event field. This type of competition shows up everywhere—in school, in church, at work, and in life in general as you run this race. That is why you need the *Training Ground*.

For the context of this chapter, I will refer to the body of Christ as the Church.

The enemy uses competition as a means to create division in the Church. The apostle Paul warns us of the competition that can occur, and he instructs us about our own selfish ambitions that we must put to rest.

> *Do nothing from selfish ambition or conceit, but in*
> *humility count others more significant than yourselves.*
>
> —Philippians 2:3

So, how does this self-ambition and competition show up in the Church? Competition shows up in those competing for the same gifts and talents. For instance, you may have three vocalists on the same worship team, and one of them competes or always tries to out-sing the others or be the first to the microphone. Another way this type of competition shows up is through the duplication of community events or ministries. An example would be if one church were to decide to give away hot meals at Thanksgiving, but then two churches on the same street decide to do the same thing at the same time in the same community. That breeds competition. Either way, it all stems from the same root: the motive of selfish ambition and conceit, to see who can sing the best or reach the most people.

Competition creates division. Competition originated from Satan. Before he was cast into the pit of hell, he was actually a beautiful angel in the heavens, wise and intelligent in his craft and the leader of worship. His heavenly name was

Lucifer. There was just one problem: Satan was so beautiful that he became prideful in his own eyes and thought he could compete against God. Ergo, he began a competition in his own heart and mind—to call himself god (Ezekiel 28; Isaiah 14). God Himself knew the true heart of Lucifer and the selfish ambition and conceit that lay beneath the surface. Because unrighteousness and sin cannot live in heaven, God cast Lucifer and a third of the angels out (Revelation 12:4). Therefore, the spirit of competition comes from the enemy himself, and he intends to create division in your ministry, your business, your marriage, your schools, your government, and the Church, all as an attack against God's Kingdom agenda. The good news is that God already conquered the grave, and victory is ours, but we still have to rid ourselves of self-ambition and conceit.

I love David's request here:

Create in me a clean heart, O God,
and renew a right spirit within me.

—Psalm 51:10

A spirit of humility—that is what we should be asking for. Wisdom seeks humility in the face of pride. Humility causes grace to cover you and blessings to chase you. Whether you have been guilty of competing against others or have fallen prey to the competitor, today simply choose humility. Receive and embrace the calling and gift with which your Creator endowed you and refine that gift.

COMPARISON

I believe that comparison is the thief of joy, and the second way the enemy seeks to destroy the Church and keep each of us from fulfilling our God-given race.

How is comparison different from competing? Comparison is when your eyes are on someone else's purpose, gifts, and talents. In your heart, you say, *Their purpose looks better than mine; I'd rather have their race than my race, their family than my family, their car than my car.* We compare jobs, status, income, kids, and churches. I have even seen Christians compare their spiritual walk with other Christians. Comparison is a sign of immaturity. Comparing yourself to someone else only fills your mind with thoughts of insecurity that say, *I'm not good enough; I will never be like that...; I might as well quit, or better yet, I might as well not even try.*

When I was growing up, my dad always compared me to other kids—especially my cousins. When he reads this, he will probably be mortified—or maybe he'll have a revelation! (*Dad, don't worry. I forgive you. I know you were comparing me because you thought it would make me better and create healthy competition for me.*) I have this one cousin in particular who was a grade older than me, and as we were growing up in school, she was (and still is!) extremely intelligent and athletic. She was part of the debate team, a straight-A student, and a cheerleader. She rocked her high school years. Me? I was just trying to find the nearest exit! My dad would constantly say, "Why don't you join the debate team like ___?"; "Why don't you make good grades like ___?" You get the picture. I hated hearing these comparison statements. It was as if nothing was ever good enough, and I felt like I had to constantly strive to do better. This only made me search for the exit route that much harder.

Comparison creates striving and insecurity, and it causes you to have to be delivered from stuff God never intended you to carry. So, parents, please stop comparing your kids to each other or to others. Now, don't worry, I love my dad and my cousin very much. Today she is an amazing, God-fearing wife who homeschools all five of her kids. She is a superwoman, and she is fulfilling God's purpose for her life.

Another form of comparison involves comparing your gifts, your talents, and your God-given purpose to someone else's. If you have ever watched a track meet, you know the track is distinctly marked with different lanes. Much like when you drive your car on the road, when you are running, you have to stay in your lane. When a runner is focused on the wrong lane, accidents happen. When you compare your God-given purpose to someone else's, you take your eyes off your calling, your future, and your gifts. This action leads to crashing into others, trips, and stumbles in your walk with Christ—and ultimately it leads to you forfeiting your own purpose, because in its current state, it doesn't look like you think it should. The apostle Paul tells us that when we compare ourselves with each other, we lack understanding (2 Corinthians 10:12). I don't want be found without an understanding of my own purpose or misunderstanding others. I desire to be found with wisdom and humility, the kind that runs alongside others and encourages them to finish well. I want to be found *co-laboring*.

CO-LABORING

Let each of you look not only to his own interests, but
also to the interests of others.

—Philippians 2:4

The ultimate *C* that combats both competing and comparison is to co-labor. Co-laboring says, "I'm in my lane, and you are in yours. How can we help each other get to the finish line?"

Co-laborers collaborate, and this is where true growth and maturity reveal themselves. To use the examples in the previous sections, when communities co-labor, they unite to create one Thanksgiving celebration, and they serve alongside each other. When worship teams co-labor, they acknowledge each other's unique gifts and acknowledge that it is God working through them on the platform and never themselves. When you co-labor, you encourage others to become better through God's Word. When you co-labor, you pray with and for the other church down the street, rather than compare it to yours. When you co-labor, you create unity and activate God's blessing in your own God-given race.

Through the last year and half of training and preparing for a full marathon, I somehow inspired a good friend of mind to also run. Why is this so important? Because she had been told by her doctors that her knees would never be fully repaired due to years of strain, and therefore she would never run. I will never forget her face when she proved them wrong by running her first two-hundred-meter race, which then led to the next

207

race of four hundred meters, to eventually her first mile-long race.

I eventually talked her into running a 10K (6.2 miles). She prepared for each race despite the challenges, and she persevered through the storms of injuries that tried to keep her from running. After months of training, the 10K race day finally arrived. It was Africa hot! Do you remember a couple of chapters back where I told you about a race in South Texas that started at noon in the heat of the day? This was that race!

As we pre-stretched to make ourselves ready, she leaned over and said, "Shannon, you don't have to stay with me. I'm going to be slow and take my time, but you can do your own thing." I bet she said that same thing to me more than ten times. I finally said, "Okay," and took off.

On mile two, I noticed three seasoned ladies who were walking. I couldn't help myself—I had to know what distance they had set out to accomplish. "The marathon relay," they replied. One of the ladies chuckled and said, "You really want to know how old we are, don't you?" Well, if they were willing to share… They were ages sixty-seven, sixty-nine, and seventy!

In that moment after speaking to these ladies who stuck together to finish together, I remembered my friend and how we were co-laboring. There was more to the race than just finishing in a certain time. This was her milestone moment, a breakthrough moment, a co-laboring moment. I ran to the halfway mark, then stopped at the aid station and waited until she arrived. We finished together because we co-labored.

Not only did my friend successfully run her second 10K, but she ran the hottest trail race in Texas, overcame the lie of the enemy, and is now preparing for her first half marathon (13.1 miles)!

When you co-labor, you inspire others. When you co-labor, you encourage others to become better. When you co-labor, you reach more people for Jesus, and you go further in your God-given race than you ever thought possible. Be an encourager. Build up those around you and watch how far you go.

Iron sharpens iron,
and one man sharpens another.

—Proverbs 27:17

TRAINING QUESTIONS

1. In what ways have you fallen into the trap of competition?

2. In what areas do you need to ask God's help with a spirit of humility?

3. To whom have you been compared, and/or to whom have you been comparing yourself?

4. Whom do you need to forgive or ask forgiveness of?

5. With whom can you co-labor this week?

MILE 17

EMBRACE THE PACE

You know what I love most? God knows the end from the beginning. His timing is perfect. His promises are "yes" and "amen." Oftentimes, we find ourselves wanting something to happen right now or come to pass sooner than what we are actually ready for. But God knows when we are ready. Just because it is taking longer than we anticipate doesn't mean it won't come to pass.

> *For still the vision awaits its appointed time; it hastens to the end—it will not lie. If it seems slow, wait for it; it will surely come; it will not delay.*
>
> *—Habakkuk 2:3*

It may seem delayed to us in the present, but it is not delayed according to God and His perfect timing. It is our responsibility to maintain our *posture* and *pace* in order to *see the people* on our journey and *run through the tape* to cross the finish line.

POSTURE

The posture of our waiting is found just a few verses before that. We find Habakkuk saying, "I will take my stand at my watchpost and station myself on the tower; and look out to see what he will say to me, and what I will answer concerning my complaint" (Habakkuk 2:1).

The word "stand" translates to *amad* in Hebrew, which means "to endure" or "to remain."[25] Wait a minute—this sounds familiar. Did we not just discuss standing firm while wearing our shoes of peace and remaining in Him? Take your stand and remain. Remain in the posture of standing. Remain surefooted while enduring, running the race you have been called to run. We're not supposed to sit on the sidelines while we wait; we are called to keep running and pressing into God's presence while we wait. Stand firm on God's Word because He is faithful.

I was recently going through a set of challenges in life, experiencing my own training ground, and I found myself wanting to sit down. I was reminded through a text message from an inner circle confidant: *Dig your pretty little heels into the ground and remain steadfast in Jesus!* In other words, remain standing. Take your stance on God's Word, believing the promises He has made and trusting you will see it come to pass. "Let us not grow weary of doing good, for in due season we will reap, if we do not give up" (Galatians 6:9). Posture your stance as one who is standing.

There are primarily two types of postures you will see runners take. A short distance sprinter will run full steam ahead with everything they have, leaning forward. On the other hand, a long-distance runner knows the journey is long, and so they will settle into a pace, remaining in an upright position, because it allows them to breathe easier and causes less stress to their back. As you run this race of life, remember it is a long-distance run, and you will breathe much easier in an upright position with your feet firmly planted on the promises of God.

PACE

Every long-distance runner knows that you have to pace yourself to finish with your goal in mind—and not everyone has the same pace. One morning I made the mental decision to run sixteen miles. That morning, I dressed for the weather, which was about 40 degrees and mildly windy. I strapped my water reservoir to my back, packed my carbohydrate snacks, cranked up the volume on my Air Pods, and started out. I began to settle into a nice pace that I knew would hold me for the next fifteen miles or so. The key to running long distances is to embrace the pace you are in so you can endure the length of the race all the way to the finish. As a long-distance runner, you cannot start the race with maximum energy and effort, or you won't have anything left in your reserves to finish well.

Each runner has his own preference on how they set his own route. I know some individuals prefer to see different scenery and not run the same route every time, whereas others are creatures of habit. I myself like to know my route ahead of time. I am a creature of habit. I run the same route and know where the mile markers are. Although I wear a watch that keeps track of my distance and route and at any time I can look at it and see just how far I have run, I prefer to know where I am by seeing land markers. This particular day, the route I chose was exactly eight miles. It doesn't take a rocket scientist to figure out I had to run that route twice to get in the number of miles I wanted to run.

After I had finished the initial eight-mile route, I thought about changing it up. Different paths and routes started to go through my mind as I was closing in on mile eight. Yet I heard the Holy Spirit say, *Run the same route.* I replied, *But, Lord, I think I want to see a different scene, something I haven't seen before.* Still the Holy Spirit brought to my remembrance the many times when the Israelites had to go around the same mountain before they would see a victory. In the book of Joshua, God commanded Joshua to march around the walls of Jericho once a day for six days, and then on the seventh day, to march around the city seven times, at which point the priests would blow the trumpets. At the sound of the trumpets, the people were to shout a great shout, and all the walls of the city would fall. Victory would be theirs.

You see, in this season of my life, I had been circling the same mountain, and I was at a breaking point. God was trying to show me what He was about to do. He was reminding me that I needed to go around it one more time, and when I was done, I was to give a great shout of victory. You better believe that as I ran the second eight-mile set, I embraced the pace and put my trust in God—that not only would I finish this run well, but that I would receive the victory for which I was fighting. I was at war. I was praying fervently with every stride, and on the completion of mile sixteen, I gave a great shout! I knew I had the victory, because God had said it.

And this is the confidence that we have toward him, that if we ask anything according to his will he hears us. And if we know that he hears us in whatever we ask, we know that we have the requests that we have asked of him.

—1 John 5:14–15

Not long after that, I ran my first full marathon of 26.2 miles. During the first half, I felt really good, and I was making great time. However, a sense of discouragement came over me as I began to see people passing me up. You see, even after you think you have conquered doubt, it still tries to sneak back in. Nevertheless, I remembered two things: I needed to maintain my posture, and I needed to embrace the pace.

The race you run in life is a marathon, not a sprint. For you to experience longevity, you must embrace the pace and know that to everything there is a season. You must train for the race you run, whether physically or spiritually. You must endure the process and pace yourself. Even though other people might pass you up—getting married before you, having kids before you do, getting promoted before you do—know that God's timing is perfect. If you will embrace His pace, endure the process of life, and use it as a training ground for your next lap, you will experience the victory!

SEE THE PEOPLE

Several years ago, I was called on to lead our outreach ministry and host an event called Elevation Backpack. This is an annual back-to-school event in which we supply kids in our community with free backpacks, school supplies, and so much more. The first time I led the event, I was running around like a crazy lady trying to make sure everyone had what they needed at each station and that our volunteers were taken care of. One of our elders at the time, who has since gone on to be with the Lord, pulled me aside. He took me to the back of the room and stood where we could view everything. I remember him putting his arm around my shoulder as we looked out across the crowd of people, then he asked, "What do you see?"

"I see a lot going on," I said.

He proceeded to ask me the same question again: "What do you see?"

"I see a lot of kids and a lot of people," I answered.

That day he left me with me these words: "See the people. I mean, *really* see the people." He was trying to get me to understand that we weren't just hosting a great event; he wanted me to see the people, to look beyond their clothes and faces, to look beyond their need. He wanted me to look into their faces and really see their joy, see their hurt, see their gratitude, see their heaviness, and see their needs being met. I never looked at that ministry in the same way. To this day, at every event and in every encounter, I try to remember to see the people, to see a little of me in them.

As I ran the full marathon, I recalled those words: "See the people." I could see not just other runners running alongside me, but I saw the people lining the roads holding signs and cheering the runners as we passed by. I saw tons of volunteers at each mile marker passing out snacks and water with an encouraging word. My eyes caught sight of a little girl who couldn't have been more than five years old at the side of the road, holding a sign that said, "Training is over—this is your victory lap!" Even as I write this, I am overwhelmed with the meaning and feeling those words bring. I can't begin to describe the joy I felt when I saw her—I had to have my photo taken with her.

In whatever you do as you run your race, don't forget to see the people—the people who will be impacted by the mark you leave on this world. Don't forget that what you do is not just for you, but it is also for someone else. Take the next generation with you and leave them something they can hold on to to run another lap. While your training for a physical race may be over, your training in life doesn't end—and every lap is a victory lap! You must fight from a stance of victory, meaning you already have the victory, you need only to possess it, and sometimes that means going around the mountain one more time. This is your victory lap!

RUN THROUGH THE TAPE

As I neared the end of my health-care career to transition into the next season of my life, I was excited, yet weary. I was making the transition in the middle of 2021, and the health-care industry had been plagued with the global pandemic of COVID-19 since 2020. In a year and a half, the entire country had shifted, the way we all did business was altered, the health-care industry was changing daily, and it was difficult to keep up with the demands. There were times when our resources were depleted, our staff were exhausted, and the well was dry. That's when I heard these words: *Shannon, run through the tape.*

As I sat across from my boss, I knew what he meant. End this season well. Give it all you've got, all the way to the end. Push through the pain, the exhaustion, the weariness, and the frustration. Run through the tape. I will never forget the day I sat across from my team to let them know that my season with them was coming to an end. Although I was excited about transitioning into my new season with anticipation of what the future held for our family, I had a mixed bag of emotions. As I looked into the faces of my team members, I could see their weariness, the heaviness of life we were all facing. I recalled the long hours they all put in, the sweat and the tears of hard work, and the labor of love we endured for each other, and for them, I knew I would run through the tape.

Have you ever noticed that when you start something new, there is a sense of excitement and anticipation, and you can't wait to get started? But then, after a while you realize you don't have the same excitement anymore. For whatever reason, there could be road blocks and obstacles that cause frustration, or storms of life that cause weariness, and you wonder if it's worth it even to keep going. The apostle Paul warned us this would happen, but he tells us to keep going, to remind ourselves how we felt when we started so that we can find that same energy and finish in the same manner that we started.

> *So now finish doing it as well, so that your readiness*
> *in desiring it may be matched by your completing it*
> *out of what you have.*
>
> —2 Corinthians 8:11

Just like when we run a physical marathon, there is exhaustion, weariness, and heaviness, but when we see the finish line, there is an excitement that rises up. This is when we realize there is a gear we didn't even know we had left to shift into. We started the race with excitement. We must remember why we started in the first place and finish with the same excitement. Run through the tape!

My fellow runner and co-laborer in Christ, thank you for running this race with me. Our journey has now come to an end. Thank you for enduring the process with me. Know that you are not alone in the seasons of life through which you are traveling. God has called you to make an impact on the next generation, to leave a legacy and fulfill your God-given purpose. I pray that you embrace the pace, finish well, finish strong, and run through the tape. Embrace the different seasons of life, trusting that your heavenly Father has your best interest at heart and knows right where you are. He is working even when you don't see it. He is moving even when you don't feel it. Even at this moment, He is adjusting divine assignments and connections for you. Stay encouraged, stay upright, stay steadfast, and keep running!

APPENDIX A

SALVATION PRAYER

Dear Lord,

Thank You for dying on the cross for me and raising from the dead to give me eternal life. Forgive me of my sins, and make me new.

From this day forward, I choose to confess that You are the Lord of my life.

In Jesus' name, amen.

If you said that simple prayer and believed it in your heart, I believe you received the gift of salvation and the Holy Spirit. Would you let us know by sending us an email?

dochaltom@gmail.com

APPENDIX B

SHANNON'S RUNNING PLAN

WEEK	SUN.	MON.	TUES.	WEDS.	THURS.	FRI.	SAT.	TOTAL
1	Rest	2	2	Rest	1	Rest	2	7
2	Rest	3	2	Rest	1	Rest	3	9
3	Rest	2	3	Rest	1	Rest	4	10
4	Rest	2	2	Rest	3	Rest	5	12
5	Rest	4	2	Rest	3	Rest	6	15
6	Rest	3	2	Rest	3	Rest	7	15
7	Rest	4	2	Rest	4	Rest	8	18
8	Rest	4	2	Rest	3	Rest	9	18
9	Rest	4	2	Rest	3	Rest	10	19
10	Rest	4	2	Rest	3	Rest	11	20
11	Rest	4	2	Rest	3	Rest	12	21
12	Rest	4	2	Rest	4	Rest	6	16
13	Rest	4	2	Rest	3	Rest	14	23
14	Rest	4	2	Rest	3	Rest	7	16
15	Rest	4	2	Rest	3	Rest	16	25
16	Rest	4	3	Rest	3	Rest	8	18
17	Rest	4	2	Rest	2	Rest	17	25

WEEK	SUN.	MON.	TUES.	WEDS.	THURS.	FRI.	SAT.	TOTAL
18	Rest	4	2	Rest	3	Rest	8	17
19	Rest	3	1	Rest	3	Rest	18	25
20	Rest	4	1	Rest	3	Rest	9	17
21	Rest	3	2	Rest	3	Rest	20	28
22	Rest	3	1	Rest	4	Rest	9	17
23	Rest	2	3	Rest	3	Rest	22	30
24	Rest	4	2	Rest	3	Rest	10	19
25	Rest	3	2	Rest	3	Rest	10	18
26	Rest	3	2	Rest	4	Rest	Rest	9
27	Rest	3	2	Rest	Rest	Rest	26.2	31.2

ABOUT THE AUTHOR

As a dynamic, energetic speaker and entrepreneur, Shannon Haltom is a Kingdom visionary who has a passion to equip others to fulfill their purpose and draw them closer to Jesus. She is a registered nurse, and she received her doctorate in nursing practice in executive leadership from Abilene Christian University in 2020.

After a successful career in the health-care industry, Shannon made a pivotal turning point to pursue her calling and purpose in life. After becoming a Maxwell Leadership Certified Team Member, she launched Run Your Race Leadership Consulting Services as a gateway to equip leaders and help organizations thrive.

Shannon is the host of "Unhindered," which airs Mondays at 2 p.m. CST on the Shannon Haltom Facebook page and YouTube channel. She loves to speak about Jesus and hopes to help others fulfill their destiny and purpose as they run their God-given race.

Shannon has served in ministry at Rescue Church since 2015, and she is passionate about community outreach and supporting the local church. She resides just south of Houston, Texas, with her husband, Bo, and two children. In her free time, she loves to trail run and spend time with her family.

NOTES

MILE 2

1 Steven Furtick, "Get Your Passion Back," April 30, 2019, https://www.youtube.com/watch?v=zZY5PpRmtqM.

2 *Merriam-Webster Dictionary*, s.v. "illuminate," accessed August 15, 2022, https://www.merriam-webster.com/dictionary/illuminate.

3 *Merriam-Webster Dictionary*, s.v. "radiate," accessed August 15, 2022, https://www.merriam-webster.com/dictionary/radiate.

MILE 4

4 John C. Maxwell, *Everyone Communicates, Few Connect* (Nashville, TN: Thomas Nelson, 2010), 48.

5 *Merriam-Webster Dictionary*, s.v. "kairos," accessed August 24, 2022, https://www.merriam-webster.com/dictionary/kairos.

MILE 6

6 Tony Evans, *The Power of God's Names* (Eugene, OR: Harvest House, 2014), 154.

MILE 7

7   T.D. Jakes, "Crushing: God Turns Pressure into Power with Bishop T.D. Jakes & Pastor Steven Furtick," April 12, 2019, https://www.youtube.com/watch?v=CzP23Zti-YI&t=4451s.

MILE 9

8   Joyce Meyer, *The Battlefield of the Mind* (New York: Hachette Book Group, 1995), 96.

9   Faith Rxd, "Passion WOD 2022," March 17, 2022, https://faithrxd.org/passionwod2022/.

MILE 10

10 Len Fisher, "How Much Salt Is in a Human Body?" Science Focus, accessed August 15, 2022, https://www.sciencefocus.com/the-human-body/how-much-salt-is-in-a-human-body/.

11 A. Bueno-Orovio, C. Sanchez, E. Pueyo, and B. Rodriguez, "Na/K pump regulation of cardiac repolarization: Insights from a systems biology approach," *PubMed* 466, no.2 (February 2014): 183–93. Doi: 10.1007/s00424-013-1293-1.

MILE 12

12 *Merriam-Webster Dictionary*, s.v. "endurance," accessed August 15, 2022, https://www.merriam-webster.com/dictionary/endurance.

13 *Hebrew Greek Key Word Study Bible*, King James Version, *hupomone*, 5281.

14 *Oxford Dictionary*, s.v. "self-discipline," accessed August 15, 2022.

15 *Merriam-Webster Dictionary*, s.v. "self-discipline," accessed August 15, 2022, https://www.merriam-webster.com/dictionary/self-discipline.

16 Daniel Goleman, *Emotional Intelligence: Why It Can Matter More than IQ* (London: Bantam Books, 1995), 12–14.

17 *Merriam-Webster Dictionary*, s.v. "resolve," accessed August 15, 2022, https://www.merriam-webster.com/dictionary/resolve.

MILE 13

18 National Institutes of Health, National Cancer Institute, "breakthrough pain," accessed August 15, 2022, https://www.cancer.gov/publications/dictionaries/cancer-terms/def/breakthrough-pain.

19 *Bible Atlas Encyclopedia*, "Baal-perazim," accessed August 15, 2022, https://bibleatlas.org/baal-perazim.htm.

MILE 14

20 *Merriam-Webster Dictionary*, s.v. "abase," accessed August 15, 2022, https://www.merriam-webster.com/dictionary/abase.

21 *Merriam-Webster Dictionary*, s.v. "abound," accessed August 15, 2022, https://www.merriam-webster.com/dictionary/abound.

MILE 15

22 Carrie Macmillan, "How to Stretch before a Run Properly," *Yale Medicine*, February 12, 2021, https://www.yalemedicine.org/news/how-to-stretch-before-run.

23 Ibid.

Brodie Sharpe, "Running & Stretching: Is There Any Benefit?" October 23, 2021, https://runsmarter.online/running-and-stretching-is-there-benefit/.

24 Logos Bible Software, "New Wineskin, Old Wineskin… What's the Difference?" 2009.

MILE 17

25 *Strong's Concordance*, "stand," *amad*, 5975, accessed August 15, 2022, https://biblehub.com/hebrew/5975.htm.